STRENGTH-BASED GOAL SETTING
in Gifted
Education

This must-have resource provides you with the tools needed to implement a strength-based approach for leading gifted and high-potential learners to Purposeful Empowerment in Goal Setting (PEGS).

Expertly developed from Gagné's (2021) DMGT Talent Development Model, PEGS incorporates self-regulation, self-reflection, and self-advocacy strategies into the goal-setting process for gifted and high-potential learners. Whether setting goals to address underachievement, twice-exceptional needs, or current or future aspirations, this book provides the guidelines and resources necessary to empower gifted learners to develop student agency and gain key insights into how their own social-emotional awareness impacts effective goal setting.

Gifted specialists, school counselors, classroom teachers, and academic coaches will find the ready-to-use forms, resources, tools, and strategies provided in this text an invaluable contribution toward their mission to guide and empower gifted and high-potential learners in the goal-setting and goal-achieving process.

Vicki Phelps, Ed.D is an Assistant Professor of Education at Milligan University. She is the recipient of the 2021 NAGC Book of the Year Award (with Emily Mofield) for *Collaboration, Coteaching, and Coaching in Gifted Education*. She has been involved in gifted education for 25 years and enjoys providing professional learning and consultation services to districts seeking to improve gifted practice.

Karah Lewis is the Lead Consulting Teacher for Gifted Education and the county-wide Gifted Consultant for high school students in Sumner County, TN. She has over 15 years of experience in the classroom and enjoys developing curriculum and strategies to support gifted students and providing professional learning opportunities for teachers.

STRENGTH-BASED GOAL SETTING
in Gifted Education

Addressing Social-Emotional Awareness, Self-Advocacy, and Underachievement in Gifted Education

Vicki Phelps and

Karah Lewis

Routledge
Taylor & Francis Group

NEW YORK AND LONDON

Cover image: © Getty Images

First published 2023
by Routledge
605 Third Avenue, New York, NY 10158

and by Routledge
4 Park Square, Milton Park, Abingdon, Oxon, OX14 4RN

Routledge is an imprint of the Taylor & Francis Group, an informa business

Library of Congress Cataloging-in-Publication Data
Names: Phelps, Vicki, author. | Lewis, Karah, author.
Title: Strength-based goal setting in gifted education : addressing social
emotional awareness, self-advocacy, and underachievement in gifted
education / Vicki Phelps and Karah Lewis.
Description: New York, NY : Routledge, 2023. |
Includes bibliographical references. |
Identifiers: LCCN 2022020769 (print) | LCCN 2022020770 (ebook) |
ISBN 9781032362687 (hardback) | ISBN 9781032362663 (paperback) |
ISBN 9781003331049 (ebook)
Subjects: LCSH: Gifted children–Education. | Goal (Psychology) |
Social learning. | Reflective learning. | Emotional intelligence. |
Academic achievement.
Classification: LCC LC3993 .P445 2023 (print) |
LCC LC3993 (ebook) | DDC 371.95–dc23/eng/20220623
LC record available at https://lccn.loc.gov/2022020769
LC ebook record available at https://lccn.loc.gov/2022020770

ISBN: 978-1-032-36268-7 (hbk)
ISBN: 978-1-032-36266-3 (pbk)
ISBN: 978-1-003-33104-9 (ebk)

DOI: 10.4324/9781003331049

Typeset in Palatino
by Newgen Publishing UK

Access the Support Material: www.routledge.com/9781032362663

To my beloved husband, David, there are not enough words to express my love for you. Your belief in me inspires me to move mountains. To my children, Brittany, Becca, and David, thank you for helping me celebrate all that life has to offer. To my dad, James, you exemplify everything I hope to be, and to my mom in heaven, your gift of words found its way to me!

–Vicki

To my wonderful husband, Josh, and my sweet daughter, Fiona, you are my world, and I am so thankful for your love and support. Thank you to my family and close friends whose help made this endeavor possible. I am truly blessed beyond belief. And to Vicki, thank you so much for seeing the value and potential in me and my work. You are an inspiration to me, and I feel blessed to have co-authored this book with you.

–Karah

Soli deo gloria

Contents

Contents

Figures

Tables

Support Material

Keep an eye out for the support material icon throughout this book, which indicates a resource is available online. Resources mentioned in this book can be downloaded, printed, used to copy/paste text, and/or manipulated to suit your individualized use.

You can access these downloads by visiting the book product page on our website: www.routledge.com/products/9781032362663. Then click on the tab that reads "Supplemental Downloads" and then select the files you need. The files will download directly to your computer.

Acknowledgments

This work never would have come to fruition without the shared experiences, challenges, and insights from our gifted and high-potential students. To all of our students past and present, thank you for showing us how being true to yourself is the greatest form of strength. To Kayren Craighead, for believing in us, sharing our vision, and recognizing the need for this program. Your belief in us has continued to grow us and stretch us in our own goal setting. Thank you to Sumner County Schools for providing a venue to explore the possibilities of Purposeful Empowerment in Goal Setting. A special thanks to Joel McIntosh for seeing the potential in our idea and launching this program into reality and to our editors for supporting us from the initial stages of project development to the final stages of publication. We are thankful for each of you!

Introduction

Regardless of whether you teach in a traditional brick and mortar classroom, an online classroom, or an alternative education setting, we all share one common goal: to empower students in their learning. It seems so simple, right? Set a goal. Achieve a goal. Repeat. All too often, however, students are viewed as knowledge receptacles awaiting their next goal and directive. As educators, we must remain mindful that each of our students is an individual with their own life experiences, strengths, values, interests, and hopes for the future. These are all key considerations when setting personalized goals that lead to student agency and add purpose to the learning process. When focusing on the academic and social-emotional needs of gifted and high-potential learners, these factors become even greater agents in the goal-setting process (Cross & Cross, 2017; Gagné, 2021; Phelps, 2022).

The Purposeful Empowerment in Goal Setting (PEGS) Model was born out of a clear and distinct need for a structure to support and grow gifted and high-potential learners in goal setting. As we searched for resources, programs, and materials specifically developed and created to involve and support gifted learners in this process, we simply could not find anything that encompassed the unique learning needs of our students. Hence, PEGS was born. From its inception, PEGS has embraced the unique life experiences of each student as a driving force in goal setting and works to leverage each student's intrapersonal awareness and interpersonal skills through a strength-based application within the educational environment. Through this *purposeful* approach, gifted and high-potential learners understand how their self-created goals are relevant to their lives both inside and outside of the school setting.

DOI: 10.4324/9781003331049-1

Equity, Standards, and Talent Development

The PEGS Model is founded on equity, the NAGC (2019) Gifted Education Programming Standards, and Gagné's (2021) Differentiating Model of Giftedness and Talent. As such, it not only recognizes the role of environment, intrapersonal awareness, and the developmental process in goal setting for gifted and high-potential learners, it explicitly integrates supports for underserved populations and provides opportunities to confront and address equitable access to purposeful and meaningful learning for every student. In addition, PEGS provides a safe space to engage in respectful discourse, explore metacognitive mindfulness, and develop self-regulation skills, which all culminate in developing student agency.

Through these inter-related dimensions of PEGS, each student begins to understand not only how their interests, strengths, and needs guide their goal-related decisions and behaviors, but also the impact of their identity, culture, beliefs, and values on their goals. For many gifted and high-potential students, this might be the first time they are given autonomy in their goal setting, allowing them the opportunity to identify what resources they may need to accomplish their goal, how they self-assess their progress, and how their goal connects to the real world outside the confines of school. By gaining these insights, students continue to grow in their ability to self-advocate, communicate effectively with others, and problem-solve through unforeseen challenges as they grow in self-confidence and self-worth.

Likewise, PEGS provides educators with a program that not only embraces the insights of gifted and high-potential learners, but also responds appropriately and purposefully to support and empower them in their learning. All in all, PEGS provides a respectful structure for gifted and high-potential students to develop self-advocacy, recognize capabilities and skills, and learn from past experiences through a strength-based approach to learning (Kane, 2020), as well as developing key psychosocial skills such as perseverance and resilience (Rimm, 2021).

About This Book

In recognizing the personalized nature of the PEGS Model and its foundation of equity and respect for every student, this book has been written with inclusive language, recognizing nonbinary pronouns throughout each chapter. The book, itself, is divided into nine chapters which span from the foundational framework of the PEGS Model to its practical applications, providing resources, activities, and step-by-step protocols.

Chapter 1 explores the foundational framework of the PEGS Model, including Gagné's (2021) Differentiating Model of Giftedness and Talent (DMGT). After outlining the need for real-world connection in goal setting, the chapter explores other driving factors behind effective goal setting for gifted and high-potential learners, including equitable talent development, motivation, psychosocial skills, respect, social-emotional awareness, specialized supports for underserved populations, strength-based pedagogy, and underachievement. The end of the chapter provides an overview connecting the PEGS Model with the NAGC (2019) Gifted Education Programming Standards through the alignment of Learning and Development, Assessment, Curriculum Planning and Instruction, Learning Environments, and Programming.

Chapter 2 discusses student agency as an anchor to the PEGS Model. After defining student agency and describing how it can be strengthened through the PEGS process, the chapter provides an introduction to the Future, Present, Past mindset of goal setting. The chapter continues by describing the integral role that value plays in the creation of purposeful and attainable goals. Likewise, self-regulation and metacognition are outlined as common threads within the PEGS Model. The chapter concludes with recognizing how to build capacity within gifted and high-potential learners through higher-order thinking skills and the goal development process.

Chapter 3 introduces the PEGS Model and gives a detailed overview of the process and stages. After discussing how the PEGS process is founded in respectful relationships, the stages of PEGS which include intrapersonal awareness, interpersonal skills, and application to the learning process are addressed. A connection is made to the goal-setting process through these lenses, and specific goal-setting scenarios are discussed. The chapter concludes by exploring how the PEGS Model is a useful tool in providing gifted and high-potential students opportunities to grow through goal setting.

Chapter 4 shares the tools used in identifying the needs of gifted and high-potential students, especially in the areas of intrapersonal awareness and interpersonal skills. Assessments in the areas of giftedness and creativity, social aptitudes, temperament, personality, motivation, task valuation, volition, and psychosocial skills are provided, along with a description of the benefits of assessing these areas. The chapter explains how these assessments are the beginning step for gifted and high-potential students in exploring where their strengths lie, where there may be barriers, and in creating goals in these areas.

Chapter 5 provides an overview of the first stage of the PEGS Model: Know Thyself. This chapter explores intrapersonal awareness within the student, the impacts of increasing this awareness, and how it connects to student agency. The *Assessments Analysis* resource first gives the student the opportunity to record and analyze the strengths and barriers discovered in Chapter 4. This chapter also provides explanations for areas of growth within intrapersonal awareness, along with activities and resources for the teacher to use with students. Areas of intrapersonal awareness addressed include social aptitudes, motivation and values, personality traits, resilience, volition, task valuation, psychosocial skills, inner dialogue, and growth mindset. Resources and activities within each area provide teachers with the tools necessary in guiding gifted and high-potential students to grow their intrapersonal strengths and overcome their barriers.

Chapter 6 expounds upon the second stage of the PEGS Model: Express Thyself. This stage focuses on interpersonal skills and the various applications of effective communication in goal setting. More specifically, the chapter provides insight, resources, and activities covering the areas of verbal/nonverbal communication, committed listening, problem-solving, conflict resolution, and adapting to new situations as key interpersonal skills associated with goal attainment. The chapter culminates with the *Effective Communication Toward Goal Development* resource, which provides a scaffold to support gifted and high-potential learners in refining their goal through newfound interpersonal skills.

Chapter 7 delves into the third stage of the PEGS Model: Apply Thyself. This stage is focused entirely on how the goal will be applied to the learning process. Students are empowered to apply what they have learned in the previous stages of PEGS to streamline how their goal will be attained and assessed. With a continued focus on Gagné's (2021) DMGT, each student's developing goal is evaluated through the lens of activities (e.g., content, access, format), investment, and progress. The chapter concludes with the *Student Self-Assessment of Progress*, which provides gifted and high-potential students an opportunity to self-assess their growth in the goal-setting process through the NAGC (2019) Gifted Education Programming Standards.

Chapter 8 details how to implement the PEGS process with students. This chapter begins by exploring the needs of gifted and high-potential students within the middle school grades and outlines the PEGS process as a beneficial tool to provide support for these students. It also discusses how the PEGS Model can be used in one-on-one teacher–student sessions, with whole group interventions and teacher–student conferencing, or in a peer-to-peer model with teacher facilitation. After its use is established, the *Purposeful Empowerment in Goal Setting Workspace* is introduced. The chapter breaks down each section of the PEGS process within this resource and describes how to implement with students. The stage of Reflection is explored in its importance and use. The chapter culminates with tips for using the PEGS Model along with examples of its success with gifted and high-potential learners.

Chapter 9 closes with exploring how the PEGS process is used at the high school level and beyond. This chapter describes the specific needs of gifted and high-potential high school students, including social-emotional characteristics, academic expectations, perfectionism, mindset, and uncertainty about the future. The chapter then explains the benefits in these areas from use of the PEGS Model with these students. There is an emphasis on communicating with stakeholders, as this impacts student agency and self-advocacy. The chapter concludes with a look at areas to focus on in each grade level of high school while using PEGS and how PEGS continues to impact gifted and high-potential students beyond high school.

How to Use This Book

One of our favorite sayings is, "Structures promote function." Without structure, there is no firm foundation or direction to support our efforts in growing and moving forward in our learning. With this in mind, the PEGS Model provides a systematic and explicit instructional model to empower gifted and high-potential students in their personalized goal setting. It is through this structure that PEGS also embraces flexibility in meeting the individualized needs of our students. In the same way that we teach our students to problem-solve and adapt to unforeseen situations, PEGS is structured to embrace flexibility in thinking and respond to diverse needs. Often, we may not even realize the needs lying beneath the surface until our students begin working through the PEGS process.

As you read this book, recognize how goal setting is not always a linear path. Often, in fact, students' most empowering goals are the manifestation of the interconnectedness of the three guiding stages of PEGS: Know Thyself, Express Thyself, Apply Thyself. While the chapters in this book introduce each stage separately, the stages often overlap. For example, while working through Apply Thyself, students often continue to grow in their intrapersonal and interpersonal awareness and skills. This is powerful as it signifies how students are connecting to and growing in their own identities. Embrace these moments, and guide students to leverage these strengths toward refining their goals. Ultimately, as gifted and high-potential students continue to grow in self-agency and goal setting, the hope is that they will also feel empowered within their own learning journey beyond high school. Celebrate the impact of gifted and high-potential students feeling confident enough in themselves that when faced with creating their own paths in the future they will live the words of Robert Frost (1979): "Two roads diverged in a wood, and I took the one less traveled by, and that has made all the difference."

References

Cross, T. L., & Cross, J. R. (2017). Social and emotional development of gifted students: Introducing the school-based psychosocial curriculum model. *Gifted Child Today*, 40(3), 178–182. https://doi.org/10.1177/1076217517713784

Frost, R. (1979). *The poetry of Robert Frost* (E. Lathem, Ed.). Holt, Rinehart and Winston.

Gagné, F. (2021). *Differentiating giftedness from talent: The DMGT perspective on talent development*. Routledge.

Kane, M. (2020). How adults can listen and respond to student voices. *Parenting for High Potential*, 9(2), 2–3.

National Association for Gifted Children. (2019). *2019 Pre-K–Grade 12 Gifted Programming Standards*. www.nagc.org/sites/default/files/standards/Intro%202019%20Programming%20Standards.pdf

Phelps, V. (2022). Motivating gifted adolescents through the power of PIE: Preparedness, innovation, and effort. *Roeper Review*, 44(1), 35–48. https://doi.10.1080/02783193.2021.2005204

Rimm, S. (2021). How parents can help gifted children gradually return to reality: Remembering our goals. *Parenting for High Potential*, 10(1), 2–3.

CHAPTER 1

Foundations of Successful Goal Setting

At the heart of every teacher lies the hopes and dreams of supporting students to become independent, problem-solving, compassionate individuals who are able to contribute to and make the world a better place. The question that remains, however, is how can this be done, especially with all of the additional complexities of life impacting the learning process and our global world?

The title of this chapter refers to *successful* goal setting, and through that simple integration of one word, there is a great deal to ponder and reflect upon. What are the various attributes that would make goal setting *successful* for our students? How can teachers ensure that goals are meaningful, purposeful, and personalized? What steps can be taken to support students in achieving their goals while also providing opportunities for continued feedback and ongoing reflection? Each of these questions becomes even more complex when taking into consideration the unique learning needs and characteristics of gifted and high-potential learners, and as such, these questions constitute the driving force behind the creation of and the need for this book.

DOI: 10.4324/9781003331049-2

Expanding Our Views of Goal Setting

Take a moment to reflect on your own goal-setting experiences as a K-12 student. What was the process you went through, or was there a process at all? Were goals "given" to you by teachers, mentors, and/or family members? As a student, did you ever hear any of the following from key adults in your life:

- ❏ Your goal for this unit of study is to earn a minimum of 14 out of 16 points on the summative assessment rubric.
- ❏ Your Individualized Education Program (IEP) goal is (insert IEP goal).
- ❏ Your goal for being part of (insert team) is to win 1st place in the next competition.
- ❏ Your goal is to achieve above x% on the benchmark assessment or pass the state-mandated standardized test.

Gifted and high-potential students often share that their school-related goals are typically focused on earning A's on various assignments, having perfect attendance, qualifying for a particular honor, or participating and excelling in various competitions. Perhaps you had similar goals throughout your own school experience. All in all, it is important to recognize that one component of *ineffective* goal setting is strictly focusing on performance outcomes. This is only compounded by focusing on goals that are assigned to, instead of created by, students.

Many years ago, a new goal-setting approach known as SMART goals was created (Doran, 1981) that slowly found its way into the education system. SMART goals *do* provide a greater understanding of personalized goal setting, as this approach helps to ensure that student-created goals are Specific, Measurable, Attainable, Realistic, and Timely. Without a doubt, each of these attributes is a key consideration for effective goal setting. These SMART goals, however, often overlook the key intrapersonal and interpersonal components that are integral in empowering students in their learning both inside and outside of the classroom.

While having an end goal in mind is imperative during the goal-setting process, it is just as important, if not more so, to recognize, re-examine, and reflect on how goals are purposefully connected to the real world (see Figure 1.1). In fact, gifted students who make connections between their self-selected goals and the society in which they live have a greater sense of purpose and are able to make greater contributions to their communities (Celik & Mertol, 2018). Through this greater awareness of "self"

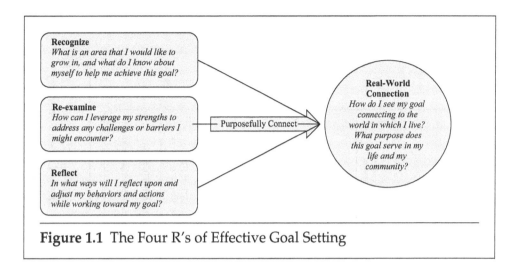

Figure 1.1 The Four R's of Effective Goal Setting

throughout the goal-setting process, gifted and high-potential learners are better able to recognize and embrace how personalized goal setting improves resiliency, purpose, and ongoing growth.

Laying the Framework for Next Steps

A strong foundation simply cannot exist without first laying a strong framework. Take for example the importance of a building's foundation. While to the naked eye it might appear to just be a giant slab of concrete ready to build a frame upon, there is much more to it than that. First, the type of soil has to be assessed as this could determine the exact type of foundation (e.g., slab on grade, pier and beam, post-tension). Upon that assessment, further decisions are made that include how to reinforce and strengthen the foundation for future construction. This, in many ways, is very similar to laying the framework for goal setting with students. We must first assess who our students are at their core. What are their backgrounds? What are their individualized needs? How have they been given, or denied, an opportunity to demonstrate their abilities? What do they value? In what ways have they been able to have ownership and student agency in their learning? What type of learning environment have they been "grown" in?

As the need for this book became more evident and we began to explore how to further empower gifted and high-potential learners through purposeful goal setting, these questions guided us to Gagné's (2021) Differentiating Model of Giftedness and Talent (DMGT; see Figure 1.2).

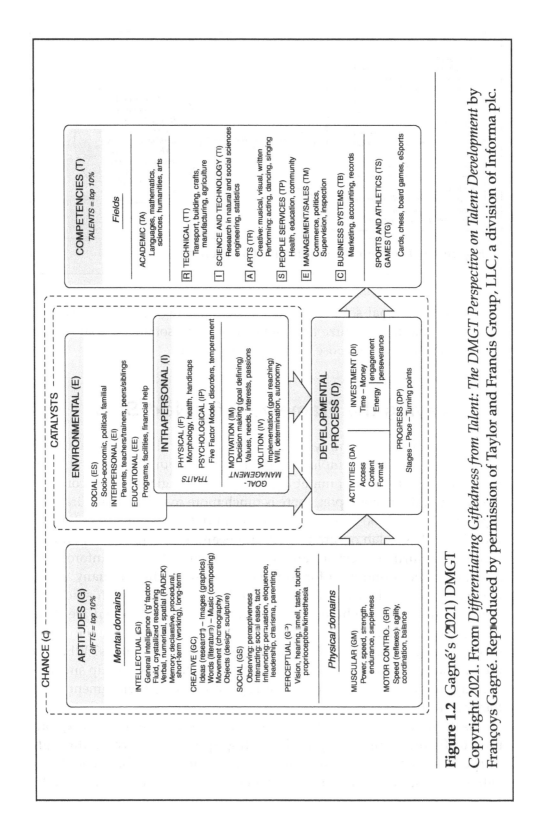

Figure 1.2 Gagné's (2021) DMGT

Copyright 2021. From *Differentiating Giftedness from Talent: The DMGT Perspective on Talent Development* by Françoys Gagné. Reproduced by permission of Taylor and Francis Group, LLC, a division of Informa plc.

It is through this framework that the Purposeful Empowerment in Goal Setting (PEGS) Model emerged and began to take root.

Growing in Goal Setting Through the DMGT

At its most basic level, Gagné's (2021) DMGT recognizes that individuals are born with aptitudes, or gifts. The DMGT illustrates how environmental factors (e.g., social constructs, interpersonal relationships, educational foundations), intrapersonal awareness (e.g., needs, values, goal setting, autonomy, determination), and the developmental process (e.g., access, content, format, investment, progress) impact the degree to which these aptitudes are developed and given the opportunity to be demonstrated as a student's talents, or competencies.

As the DMGT is applied to goal setting, one must ask, "How can the different components of the DMGT be leveraged to further support and empower gifted and high-potential learners to set purposeful goals and provide a meaningful structure to support them in achieving those goals?" Table 1.1 provides a greater context for how the DMGT components closely relate to the goal-setting process.

As connections between the DMGT and PEGS are further explored and made explicit, one also begins to recognize how these understandings subsequently open the door to other driving factors behind effective goal setting (see Table 1.2). While each of these factors could constitute full chapters, the following sections provide a brief overview of their connection to the goal-setting process for gifted and high-potential learners.

Equitable Talent Development

Talent development is defined as "the progressive transformation of high-level aptitudes into outstanding competencies, with the constant (positive or negative) influence of two important sets of catalysts: intrapersonal and environmental" (Gagné, 2021, p. 94). When considering equitable talent development through the DMGT lens, it continues to emphasize the importance placed on the intrapersonal awareness and interpersonal skills necessary to navigate one's environment (Chan & Yuen, 2013). The similarities to goal setting are evident, since recognizing one's personal needs and strengths and learning how to communicate those needs are indeed catalysts to achieving one's goals.

TABLE 1.1

Connections to Goal Setting Through the DMGT

DMGT Catalyst	Attributes	Goal-Setting Connections
Aptitudes/Gifts (G)	• Intellectual • Creative • Social • Perceptual • Muscular • Motor Control	• Recognizes that all students have aptitudes that can be cultivated • Provides a context for incorporating aptitudes through a strength-based approach to goal setting • Acknowledges there are catalysts that impact the development of aptitudes into talents/competencies through the goal-setting process • Recognizes the diversity in gifts and aptitudes that can be strengthened through the goal-setting process

Environmental (E)	• Social
	  o Socio-economic status
	  o Familial
	• Interpersonal
	  o Parents
	  o Teachers/Trainers
	  o Peers/Siblings
	• Educational
	  o Programs
	  o Facilities
	  o Financial
		• Acknowledges the impact of societal constraints on goal acquisition
		• Recognizes the role of parents, teachers, and peers on setting and achieving one's goals
		• Integrates interpersonal skills as a catalyst to achieving one's goals
		• Provides an opportunity to learn how to communicate one's needs
		• Incorporates how educational programming (e.g., pacing, grouping, curricula) can influence and impact goal attainment

Intrapersonal (I)	• Motivation
	  o Decision-making
	  o Values
	  o Needs
	  o Interests
	  o Passions
	• Volition
	  o Implementation
	  o Will
	  o Determination
	  o Autonomy
		• Makes the goal-setting process personalized and unique to each individual
		• Serves as a tool to understand one's needs in order to recognize what goals should be defined
		• Strengthens self-advocacy
		• Signifies the importance of goal-defining and goal-attainment attributes

TABLE 1.1 (Continued)

Connections to Goal Setting Through the DMGT

DMGT Catalyst	Attributes	Goal-Setting Connections

Developmental Process (D)	• Activities
	  ○ Access
	  ○ Content
	  ○ Format
	• Investment
	  ○ Time
	  ○ Energy (i.e., engagement, perseverance)
	• Progress
	  ○ Stages
	  ○ Pace
	  ○ Turning Points
		• Serves as the connection between the student-created goal and the application to the learning process
		• Provides a route through which goal attainment can be measured and quantified
		• Recognizes how access contributes to goal attainment
		• Signifies the priority of time and energy to supporting the goal-setting process
		• Outlines the goal-setting process through stages, pace, and turning points

Competencies/ Talents (T)	• Academic • Technical • Science & Technology • Arts • People Services • Management/Sales • Business Systems	• Provides a context to measure the impact of the goal on student growth across multiple areas

Note: Adapted from Gagne (2021).

TABLE 1.2

Driving Factors Behind Effective Goal Setting for Gifted Learners

• Equitable talent development • Motivation • Psychosocial skills • Respect	• Social-emotional awareness • Specialized supports for underserved populations • Strength-based pedagogy • Underachievement

The DMGT also recognizes equitable access as a key component of the developmental process. Specifically, if gifted and high-potential students have limited access to learning resources, then their ability to demonstrate their talents will be impacted. In regard to goal setting, this becomes a driving factor, since students need to be given the opportunity to leverage their life experiences, or funds of knowledge, as they set goals and work to achieve them (Ford et al., 2022). This, again, recognizes the importance of intrapersonal awareness and environmental factors within talent development and goal setting.

As gifted and high-potential learners are provided equitable access to learning and resources, their schema, or background knowledge, will continue to grow. As their schema grows, they will be better equipped to recognize, re-examine, and reflect (see Figure 1.1) upon purposeful connections and contributions to the global world. In turn, as gifted and high-potential students are empowered through goal setting, there is also a positive effect on their academic success (Celik & Mertol, 2018). In addition, the process of transforming natural abilities into talents is focused on long-term learning that can be directly impacted by student-driven goals (Chan & Yuen, 2013).

Motivation

Without question, motivation plays a large role in setting and achieving meaningful and personalized goals. When focusing on motivation of gifted and high-potential students, in particular, it is important to note that gifted learners have been found to have higher levels of intrinsic and extrinsic motivation as compared to their non-gifted counterparts, leading them to higher levels of cognitive mastery (Abu-Hamour & Al-Hmouz, 2013; Agaliotis & Kalyva, 2019; Clinkenbeard, 2012; Gottfried & Gottfried, 2004; Gur Erdogan & Yurtkulu, 2017). How, then, can motivation be leveraged to further engage gifted and high-potential learners in the goal-setting process?

With motivation being a key factor behind a gifted learner's success (Chan & Yuen, 2013), a greater understanding of the meaning of motivation within the DMGT further substantiates its impact on goal setting. Gagné (2021) recognizes that motivation stems from Action Control Theory (Corno, 1993) in that the pursuit of goals is broken down into a pre-decisional phase, which focuses on the identification and justification of goals, and a post-decisional phase, which focuses on the necessary efforts to achieve the goal. Within the pre-decisional phase, there is an intentional focus on intrapersonal awareness, including beliefs, values, needs, interests, avoidance, and approaches to achieve the goal. Likewise, during the post-decisional phase, there is a focus on how the goal can be achieved within a given environment, including the interpersonal skills needed to communicate and navigate toward attaining the established goal. Providing opportunities for gifted and high-potential learners to recognize these different components of goal setting continues to give greater purpose to the goal (Celik & Mertol, 2018) while also encouraging autonomy within the process (Gagné, 2021). Without buy-in of the goal's purpose and a clear, personal connection to the goal, there is a greater chance for underachievement to become more prevalent in gifted and high-potential learners.

Psychosocial Skills

Well-developed psychosocial skills are at the core of achieving one's goals. These consist of skills such as time management, reflection, responding positively to setbacks, perseverance, setting long-term and short-term goals, and working collaboratively, to name a few. It is essential for gifted and high-potential learners to have ongoing opportunities to develop these skills as they continue to work toward their potential (Cross & Cross, 2017), so providing a structure to develop, monitor, and reflect upon these goals is paramount.

One of the first steps in encouraging psychosocial development is to guide gifted students in learning more about their strengths and areas for growth. The intrapersonal awareness gained from working through this process continues to support students in making well-informed decisions for future goals, increase the value they place on goals, and enhance the organizational skills needed to achieve their goals (Agaliotis & Kalyva, 2019). Likewise, as gifted and high-potential learners are supported through the goal-setting process, their psychosocial skills will be strengthened, leading to greater success across all domains (Subotnik et al., 2011).

Respect

Respectful relationships are another integral component of the goal-setting process. Respecting someone means giving due regard or consideration to the other person and their ideas. When we think of the role respect plays for gifted and high-potential learners, it can manifest in three separate areas of their lives: respect between teacher and student, respect between the student and themself, and respect the student shows in outside interactions. Each of these should be cultivated within the goal-setting process.

Gifted and high-potential students have advanced abilities to understand complex concepts and events, which lead them to seek out relationships with adults (Rakow, 2020). This can increase the student's desire to talk with teachers and hold more stake in their guidance. However, teachers can quickly deter a student from opening up to them if the teacher has not created a respectful environment. Teachers looking to encourage students to build the skills needed to become successful, empowered adults should regularly treat students fairly, show students respect in all situations, and communicate in such a way that students give the same respect back to the teacher (Tischler & Vialle, 2009).

When the teacher and student relationship is securely based in respect, the teacher can then encourage the student to show respect for themself and for others. Many gifted and high-potential students experience rigorous expectations from themselves, teachers, parents, and peers. Negative self-talk, self-criticism, and imperfection can be created if students have difficulty navigating these expectations (Rakow, 2020). Teachers can guide students to set goals for developing a self-respecting inner dialogue that will increase their self-esteem, self-efficacy, and motivation. This respectful self-talk will then in turn guide their relationships and interpersonal communication. When students receive respect and show respect for themselves and others, their ownership of the goal-setting process will increase, and positive outcomes will occur.

Strength-Based Pedagogy

When working with gifted and high-potential learners to set purposeful and meaningful goals, it is important to work through a strength-based approach. As learners, we all have our strengths and weaknesses, and it is important that we continue to learn how to work through our strengths to achieve our goals. This might be leveraging our ability to communicate effectively to resolve conflict, to adapt to unforeseen challenges that arise over time, or to think analytically to solve a problem.

Quite often, goals are focused on strengthening or improving a current standing. For example, a goal might focus on improving study skills, achieving a higher level of mastery, or effectively managing one's time. Regardless of the focus, it is easy to fall into the trap of focusing on the challenges associated with achieving that goal. By recognizing how to leverage one's strengths to approach the goal, the task becomes less daunting, so it is imperative that teachers provide gifted and high-potential learners with ongoing opportunities to recognize their intelligence and abilities as they navigate this process.

Social-Emotional Awareness

Social-emotional awareness is another consideration in the goal-setting process. In knowing that a student's giftedness may impact how a student experiences events or challenges (Cross & Cross, 2015), it becomes even more important to acknowledge the role of intrapersonal awareness and the environment within the social-emotional realm. When working through this process with gifted and high-potential learners, be particularly mindful of students' levels of stress, social difficulties, anxiety, and isolation (Bakar & Ishak, 2014; Cross & Cross, 2015) as these are areas in which gifted students might need additional support. While Gagné's (2021) DMGT may not specifically mention these various attributes, it does readily acknowledge that social-emotional triggers may negatively impact engagement with any given learning task and impact the pathway to achieving one's goals.

Specialized Supports for Underserved Populations

Recognizing historically underserved populations in gifted education and how to best support them in the goal-setting process is paramount. These racially, culturally, ethnically, and linguistically diverse (RCELD) students have often not received the appropriate supports to nurture their gifts into talents. As such, it is imperative that teachers provide a sense of belongingness to RCELD students. Through this belongingness, students will feel more supported and empowered to face any challenges that might arise while working to achieve their goals (Floyd & Roberson, 2021). In addition, scaffolds might be needed to support RCELD students in creating and communicating their personalized goals. These supports might include providing extra visuals, opportunities to connect to their funds of knowledge, and/or sentence stems such as:

- ❏ I recognize one of my strengths to be _____.
- ❏ I would like to focus on improving _____.
- ❏ Something I value is _____.

In addition, remain mindful of having culturally responsive materials in the classroom that signify prominent RCELD individuals and how they have achieved their goals. In doing so, every student, gifted or non-gifted, will have the opportunity to see how successful people of all backgrounds set goals and persevere to achieve them.

Another underserved population within gifted education is twice-exceptional learners. Twice-exceptional learners are students who have two or more exceptionalities that impact their learning, with one of these exceptionalities being giftedness and the other coexisting exceptionality being from the 14 disabilities as recognized by the Individuals with Disabilities Education Act (IDEA, 1990). When working with this population of students, it is important to note that their skills in self-regulation and goal setting, in general, are typically lower than their gifted counterparts (Stankovska & Rusi, 2014). As such, these students require greater supports to develop those skills while also continuing to develop intrapersonal awareness and interpersonal skills.

Additional barriers that might need to be addressed when working with twice-exceptional learners include their acute awareness of their difficulties in learning, generalized feelings of inadequacy, avoidance behaviors, and feelings of frustration with setting and achieving goals (Stankovska & Rusi, 2014). As with any gifted learner, there is not one twice-exceptional learner who is identical to the next, so remain mindful of setting meaningful and personalized goals that leverage each student's individual strengths and provide frequent and purposeful feedback and guidance throughout the goal-setting process.

Underachievement

Underachievement is when there is a significant discrepancy between a child's ability (e.g., expected achievement) and the child's current level of practice (e.g., actual achievement). Underachievement in gifted learners is often caused by setting unrealistic goals that lack goal-directed behaviors and stems from a fear of failure and/or success (Reis & McCoach, 2000). It is important to raise awareness as to how to best support students who fall into this realm. First and foremost, gifted and high-potential learners need to recognize and believe in their intellectual strengths and talents (Peterson, 2009). This, again, acknowledges the importance of intrapersonal awareness. Likewise, gifted underachieving students also tend to have weaker social skills as compared to their high-achieving gifted peers (Agaliotis & Kalyva, 2019). This impacts the degree to which they might seek help or self-advocate for their needs. When addressing goal setting with this population, a focus on self-advocacy through developing interpersonal skills must be a priority. This connection to the personal needs of gifted and high-potential learners is also clearly related to school success

(Clinkenbeard, 2012), which further aligns Gagné's (2021) DMGT as the framework for the PEGS Model.

Making Goals a Reality

While this chapter has primarily focused on the theoretical foundations of the PEGS Model, it is equally important, if not more so, to understand the connections between these foundations and the reality of teaching gifted and high-potential learners within a classroom setting. Regardless of whether instruction is taking place in a traditional classroom, through distance learning, or through homeschooling or alternative learning environments, PEGS is further strengthened by its alignment with the National Association for Gifted Children's (NAGC, 2019) Gifted Education Programming Standards. By recognizing how PEGS is supported through these standards, the practical application of this model is further strengthened.

As this chapter concludes, Table 1.3 provides a brief overview connecting the NAGC (2019) Gifted Education Programming Standards to the PEGS Model. We also encourage you to reference these standards in their entirety as a guiding framework within your own instructional practice.

TABLE 1.3

Connections Between PEGS Model and NAGC (2019) Gifted Education Programming Standards

NAGC (2019) Gifted Education Programming Standards	Connections to Purposeful Empowerment in Goal Setting (PEGS)
Standard 1: Learning and Development	• Provides opportunities for students to understand how their interests, strengths, and needs guide goal-related decisions • Provides opportunities for students to understand how their identity, culture, beliefs, and values guide goal-related decisions • Explicitly integrates respect as a means to understand similarities and differences between students, teachers, peer groups, and others as a driving force in goal-related decisions

(continued)

TABLE 1.3 (Continued)
Connections Between PEGS Model and NAGC (2019) Gifted
Education Programming Standards

NAGC (2019) Gifted Education Programming Standards	Connections to Purposeful Empowerment in Goal Setting (PEGS)
	• Provides significant opportunities to further develop cognitive growth and psychosocial skills through goal setting that support an equitable approach to talent development • Clearly connects the goal-setting process with future career goals and aspirations and the subsequent resources needed to achieve them
Standard 2: Assessment	• Incorporates a variety of assessments to identify students' interests, natural talents, and values that recognize and respect students from diverse backgrounds • Provides frequent opportunities for students to self-assess their progress in achieving their goals
Standard 3: Curriculum Planning and Instruction	• Supports educators as they plan instruction focused on developing academic, social-emotional, and psychosocial skills involved in goal setting and goal attainment • Incorporates resources and materials for educators to use as they guide students to connect goals to a diverse and global society • Creates consistent and ongoing opportunities to develop student agency by supporting students in independent goal setting
Standard 4: Learning Environments	• Provides opportunities for students to demonstrate growth in self-awareness, self-advocacy, self-efficacy, confidence, motivation, resilience, independence, curiosity, and risk-taking • Develops ongoing opportunities to develop and apply effective interpersonal skills
Standard 5: Programming	• Provides an instructional framework with supporting resources to support students in their cognitive, social-emotional, and psychosocial learning and growth

References

Abu-Hamour, B., & Al-Hmouz, H. (2013). A study of gifted high, moderate, and low achievers in their personal characteristics and attitudes toward school and teachers. *International Journal of Special Education, 28*(3), 5–15.

Agaliotis, I., & Kalyva, E. (2019). Motivational differences of Greek gifted and non-gifted high-achieving and gifted under-achieving students. *International Education Studies, 12*(2). https://doi.org/10.5539/ies.v12n2p45

Bakar, A. Y., & Ishak, N. M. (2014). Counseling services for Malaysian gifted students: An initial study. *International Journal for the Advancement of Counseling, 36*(4), 372–383. https://doi.org/10.1007/s10447-014-9213-4

Celik, N. D., & Mertol, H. (2018). Gifted students' purpose in life. *Universal Journal of Educational Research, 6*(10), 2210–2216. https://doi.org/10.13189/ujer.2018.061019

Chan, R., & Yuen, M. (2013). Factors influencing talent development: Stories of four Hong Kong elite sportspersons. *Gifted and Talented International, 28*(1–2), 123–134. https://doi.org/10.1080/15332276.2013x.11678408

Clinkenbeard, P. R. (2012). Motivation and gifted students: Implications of theory and research. *Psychology in the Schools, 49*(7), 622–630. https://doi.org/10.1002/pits.21628

Corno, L. (1993). The best-laid plans: Modern conceptions of volition and educational research. *Educational Researcher, 22*, 11–22.

Cross, T. L., & Cross, J. R. (2015). Clinical and mental health issues in counseling the gifted individual. *Journal of Counseling & Development, 93*, 163–172. https://doi.org/10.1002/j.1556-6676.2015.00192.x

Cross, T. L., & Cross, J. R. (2017). Social and emotional development of gifted students: Introducing the school-based psychosocial curriculum model. *Gifted Child Today, 40*(3), 178–182. https://doi.org/10.1177/1076217517713784

Doran, G. T. (1981). There's a S.M.A.R.T. way to write management's goals and objectives. *Management Review, 70*, 35–36.

Floyd, E. F., & Roberson, J. J. (2021). Anxiety and the social emotional needs of minoritized gifted students. *Teaching for High Potential*, 4–5.

Ford, D. Y., Collings, K. H., & Grantham, T. C. (2022). Addressing gifts and talents, racial identity, and social-emotional learning regarding students of color: Challenges and recommendations for culturally responsive practice. In S. K. Johnson, D. Dailey, & A. Cotabish (Eds.), *NAGC Pre-K-Grade 12 Gifted Education Programming*

Standards: A guide to planning and implementing quality services (2nd ed., pp. 58–93). Routledge. https://doi.org/10.4324/978100 3236863-3

Gagné, F. (2021). *Differentiating giftedness from talent: The DMGT perspective on talent development*. Routledge.

Gottfried, A. E., & Gottfried, A. W. (2004). Toward the development of a conceptualization of gifted motivation. *Gifted Child Quarterly, 48*(2), 121–132. https://doi.org/10.1177/001698620404800205

Gur Erdogan, D., & Yurtkulu, T. (2017). Perceptions of gifted and non-gifted students related to their levels of self-actualization. *Eurasian Journal of Educational Research, 68,* 203–220. https://doi.org/10.14689/ejer.2017.68.11

Individuals With Disabilities Education Act, 20 U.S.C. §1401 et seq. (1990). https://sites.ed.gov/idea/statuteregulations

National Association for Gifted Children. (2019). *2019 Pre-K–Grade 12 Gifted Programming Standards*. www.nagc.org/sites/default/files/standards/Intro%202019%20Programming%20Standards.pdf

Peterson, J. S. (2009). Myth 17: Gifted and talented individuals do not have unique social and emotional needs. *Gifted Child Quarterly, 53*(4), 280–282. https://doi.org/10.1177/0016986209346946

Rakow, S. (2020). *Educating gifted students in Middle School*. Routledge.

Reis, S. M., & McCoach, D. B. (2000). The underachievement of gifted students: What do we know and where do we go? *Gifted Child Quarterly, 44*(3), 152–170. https://doi.org/10.1177/001698620004400302

Stankovska, G., & Rusi, M. (2014). Cognitive, emotional and social characteristics of gifted students with learning disability. *Higher Education, Lifelong Learning and Social Inclusion, 4,* 438–442.

Subotnik, R. F., Olszewski-Kubilius, P., & Worrell, F. C. (2011). Rethinking giftedness and gifted education: A proposed direction forward based on psychological science. *Psychological Science in the Public Interest, 12*(1), 3–54. https://doi.org/10.1177/1529100611418056

Tischler, K., & Vialle, W. J. (2009). Gifted students' perceptions of the characteristics of effective teachers. In D. Wood (Ed.), *The gifted challenge: Challenging the gifted* (pp. 115–124). NSWAGTC Inc.

CHAPTER 2

Student Agency as a Driving Force

While understanding the foundations of goal setting is important, one must also remain cognizant of the structures that need to be in place to achieve these goals. Later chapters will discuss the various scaffolds, tools, and steps that can be put in place to support students in this process, but first and foremost, gifted and high-potential learners need to feel connected to and take ownership of the goals that are being created. As such, Purposeful Empowerment in Goal Setting (PEGS) is anchored in student agency.

Student agency is centered on each individual recognizing how the task at hand is connected to their own life, finding value in the task, and accepting responsibility to do their personal best to achieve that task. In short, student agency is "a student's desire, ability, and power to determine their own course of action, whether that means choosing a learning goal, a topic to study, an activity to pursue, or a means of pursuing it" (Vaughn, 2018, p. 63). In this context, the PEGS Model focuses on creating student agency through the process of purposeful goal setting.

Student agency goes well beyond the "voice and choice" that is often found within gifted classrooms. By developing student agency through the goal-attainment process, gifted and high-potential students are given the opportunity to develop the "intentionality and forethought to derive a course of action and adjust the course as needed to reflect one's identity,

DOI: 10.4324/9781003331049-3

competencies, knowledge and skills, mindsets, and values" (Nagaoka et al., 2015, p. 6). While intrapersonal awareness, interpersonal skills, and environmental factors play a large role in this, there are other factors that must be considered when developing goals through the student agency mindset.

Vaughn (2018) describes student agency as having three unique dimensions: disposition, motivational, and positional. The disposition aspect deals with the descriptive qualities of the individual. When dealing with gifted and high-potential learners, the National Association for Gifted Children (NAGC) recognizes these characteristics might include descriptors such as creative, enthusiastic, self-aware, abstract thinker, questioning, intense, impulsive, and talkative (Clark, 2008). Through the PEGS Model, a greater awareness of each individual's traits will also become more evident. Secondly, motivation is another aspect of student agency in that it instills the belief that each individual is capable when placed in a situation that they believe in. Bandura (1989) refers to this as self-efficacy, or the ability to make plans, self-regulate emotions and behavior, and reflect on one's own skills. When considering goal setting through this lens, gifted and high-potential students continue to learn how to control and direct their beliefs and emotions to complete tasks and work toward achieving goals effectively. Finally, the third aspect of student agency focuses on how individuals position themselves within groups, organizations, and communities. This area is intently focused on one's social, cultural, and historical environment (Vygotsky, 1978; Wenger, 1998). This is also an area of goal setting which allows the student to recognize their own sense of identity within the context of our global world, further solidifying a greater purpose behind goal setting. While each of these components is an integral piece of student agency, the true power comes from the integration of all three dimensions working together across time.

Recognizing Student Agency Across Time

All too often, goal setting can lead people to focus on the past. Perhaps it is reflecting on what they should have done differently to take an alternate path, wondering how outcomes might have changed if different decisions were made, or being lost in the world of what-ifs. While being reflective is powerful and purposeful, it is not meant to anchor us in the past. Rather, it is meant to support us in modifying behaviors, making changes, and evolving into better versions of ourselves as we move into the future.

The PEGS Model focuses on goal setting through the Future, Present, Past mindset (Poon, 2018). Through this approach, goal setting *begins* with looking forward to identify where one desires to be or what someone wants to achieve. This raises awareness of setting an advantageous goal which will have a positive impact on one's future. Once this goal is established, goal setting is then examined through the "present" context, including identifying what current steps need to be taken to initiate action toward the future-minded goal. Finally, an individual reflects on past behaviors, barriers, and successes that will provide insight in moving forward and regulating progress toward achieving their goal. Table 2.1 provides questions to guide students in the Future, Present, Past mindset.

Goal setting through the Future, Present, Past mindset allows students to be forward-thinking in goal setting vs. focusing on any past behaviors that might inhibit them from moving forward. While this provides a

TABLE 2.1

Questions to Guide Students in Goal Setting Through the Future, Present, Past Mindset

Goal-Setting Stage	Question Stems
Future This initial stage of goal setting is focused on what one would like to accomplish in the future.	• What is something you would like to accomplish this year? • What would you like to improve upon in your academic learning? • What would be helpful to focus on when preparing for next year?
Present This initial stage of goal setting is focused on initiating action toward the goal.	• Who are people you will need to communicate with to achieve this goal? • What barriers might need to be addressed to achieve this goal? • How might you leverage your strengths in working toward this goal?
Past This initial stage of goal setting is focused on reflection as a means to regulate progress in moving forward.	• What similar goals have you set for yourself in the past, and how can you apply what you learned from those experiences? • In reflecting on past behaviors, how will you hold yourself accountable and monitor your progress while working to achieve this goal? • How have you had to adapt to unforeseen challenges in the past, and how might those skills support you in achieving this goal?

Note: Adapted from Poon (2018).

proactive approach to creating student agency in goal setting with gifted and high-potential learners, the PEGS Model, as discussed in the following chapters, will continue to provide a systematic, explicit process to further empower students through the steps needed to develop their purposeful goals.

The Value in the Process

Another significant factor in creating student agency is creating value in the process for gifted and high-potential learners. Simply stated, if students do not recognize the value behind the purpose of the goal, then they will not engage and take ownership in achieving that goal. Cash (2016) outlines key considerations in creating this value by making goals attainable, interesting, and useful. Keep in mind that these are conversations teachers have with students as they are creating their own goals, and it is through this ownership that value continues to increase, leading to greater feelings of personal empowerment within the process.

Creating value in goal setting is further enhanced by recognizing how gifted and high-potential learners value tasks based on their own personal task valuation measures. Wigfield and Eccles (2002) examine how task valuation is increased when students believe there is a direct or indirect benefit that will be achieved from completing a task. When goals are associated with one's identity, interests, and future aspirations, there is a greater chance that students will persevere, avoid distractions, and monitor their progress while working toward their goals.

When working to increase task valuation in goal setting, it is essential to guide gifted and high-potential learners through the process of identifying their own core values. This can be done by identifying people they admire, understanding the positive character traits those people have, and recognizing how the core values are exemplified through their behaviors and actions. Chapter 4 provides additional resources to support students in learning what they value and recognizing the value within their goals.

Self-Regulation as a Key to Success

Throughout this chapter there have been several references to self-regulated learning (SRL) within the context of student agency. First and foremost, student agency and SRL are not constructs unique to gifted education, as they are practices that benefit each and every student. As discussed in Chapter 1, through equitable talent development, there should also be a consistent focus on providing every student with opportunities to advance and grow in their learning through equitable access to new experiences, strategies, content, and applications of learning. With this understanding, one is better equipped to recognize giftedness in those yet to be identified, while also addressing the unique motivational and academic needs of this population.

SRL also provides the context to support students who may not be working up to their potential (e.g., underachievers, twice-exceptional learners) while also continuing to move students who have demonstrated content mastery to more advanced levels of learning. At its core, SRL refers to the process by which learners are able to personally activate and sustain their thinking, feelings, and actions toward the attainment of learning goals (Schunk & Zimmerman, 2012). Gagné (2021) recognizes that SRL places the focus on the learner, especially in regard to cognitive and metacognitive processes. This, again, continues to grow student agency in gifted and high-potential learners while developing the positive dispositions resulting from self-regulation. See Table 2.2 for traits of self-regulated learners.

When developing these skills in gifted and high-potential learners, Cash (2016) introduces the ABC's (i.e., Affect, Behavior, Cognition) of SRL. Through this process, students identify their feelings, actions, and thinking associated with the goals that are being developed (see Table 2.3). As a result, student agency is strengthened, and gifted and high-potential learners are more apt to:

❏ Set more challenging goals in the future
❏ Take responsibility in their learning
❏ Maintain engagement within the goal-attainment process
❏ Welcome challenges as new opportunities for growth
❏ Expend ongoing, sustainable effort over extended periods of time
❏ Self-advocate when necessary
❏ Develop persistence, tenacity, and resilience

TABLE 2.2

Characteristics and Traits of Self-Regulated Learners

A self-regulated learner is one who... • Utilizes effective coping strategies • Recognizes distractions • Maximizes levels of performance • Uses effective study habits • Seeks support when necessary	• Sets clear goals • Expends effort • Is aware of what is needed to be successful

TABLE 2.3

Questions to Develop Self-Regulated Skills in Gifted Learners

Self-Regulation Attribute	Question Stems to Develop SRL
Affect What is the student *feeling* in regard to their goal?	• What excites you about this goal and how can that excitement be leveraged? • What aspects of this goal feel overwhelming, and how might supports be developed to alleviate that stress? • How attentive do you feel toward achieving this goal? Are there adjustments that need to be made to increase your level of attention? • What feelings from past experiences might come to the surface while working to achieve this goal? Are there feelings that need to be addressed?
Behaviors What are the student's *actions* toward achieving their goal?	• What work habits will you be able to implement to achieve this goal? • How will you communicate with others throughout this process? • How might you need to self-advocate while working to achieve this goal? • What are some ways that you might overcome barriers during this process?
Cognition How is the student *thinking* through the various components needed to achieve their goal?	• What are you thinking in terms of your plan for achieving this goal? • In what ways will you be thinking about your progress toward meeting this goal? • What thinking strategies might you incorporate to support you in this process? • How will you evaluate and integrate new information throughout this process?

Note: Adapted from Cash (2016).

Metacognitive Mindfulness

Metacognition, or thinking about one's thinking, is a key component within the PEGS Model. While Chapter 3 provides a strong overview of the model before sharing more about the application of PEGS in subsequent chapters, it is also important to point out the significance of metacognition within the goal-setting process. First and foremost, gifted learners are conceptual thinkers, often exploring the big idea behind their learning. This ability to think more abstractly and conceptually is also closely tied to the ability to think metacognitively.

At its roots, metacognition is a culmination of thinking about one's knowledge and experiences, as well as beliefs of self, strategies, and cognitive functions. These metacognitive experiences are a combination of affective and conscious experiences that are accompanied by and related to intellectual enterprise (Flavell, 1979). A key component of metacognitive thinking is the use of mental models. Basically, mental models are a set of beliefs that are formed from one's own experiences, and thus, guide thoughts and behaviors to deeper understanding. We refer to these mental models as metacognitive thinking tools.

Metacognitive thinking tools provide a greater context for gifted and high-potential learners to remain mindful of where they are cognitively while working to achieve their goals. Not only do these thinking tools continue to develop student agency in goal setting, the "mindfulness" associated with using these tools has also been found to have a positive impact on gifted students' learning, as well as on how they see and interact with the world (Sisk, 2021). The following examples of metacognitive thinking tools might be used as a component of exit tickets, questions to guide conversations in building intrapersonal and interpersonal awareness, or reflection tasks associated with applying goal-related outcomes to the learning process:

❏ **Anchoring:** Through anchoring, students recognize any "heavy thoughts" that are either holding them back from successfully moving forward with their goals or, to the contrary, providing a strong tether to keep them "anchored" in the mission at hand and not veering off track. When working with gifted and high-potential learners in understanding this metacognitive thinking tool, it is important for them to address any biases they might have in place, assumptions related to their goal, or their core understandings of key components of their goal. A guiding question to address anchoring is, "How is your thinking about your goal affected by an 'anchoring' thought from your background and life experiences?"

❏ **Reverse Routing:** In reverse routing, gifted and high-potential students work backwards from their goal. With the end goal in mind, students are able to systematically create a plan that connects what they want to achieve back to where they currently are in regard to achieving that goal. This thinking tool is centered on goal achievement and focuses on such factors as time management, prioritization, and breaking down larger steps into smaller, more manageable tasks. A guiding question to connect students with this metacognitive thinking tool might be something as simple as, "How might you think about working backwards from what you hope to achieve in your goal to create a plan of action?"

❏ **Committed Cognition:** Through the metacognitive thinking tool of committed cognition, gifted and high-potential learners process the consistency and commitment in their thinking to achieve their self-created goal. Again, launching into this mind model with students might begin with a question such as, "In thinking about your goal, in what ways have you been consistent in your thinking? In what ways have you been inconsistent?"

❏ **Peer Pressure Pathways:** Through peer pressure pathways, gifted and high-potential students think about how their processing of information in regard to their goal is impacted by their interactions with peers or significant individuals in their lives. Are there any potential unconscious biases that might be affecting their path to success because of fear of judgment from peers? Are they more motivated because of wanting to outperform their peers? These are key considerations of how outside factors can impact personal thinking processes. A potential question through this metacognitive thinking tool might be, "How is your metacognition about your goal impacted by others' perceptions of you or your goal?"

While these are just a sample of metacognitive thinking tools, they provide opportunities for gifted and high-potential learners to recognize how mental models continue to raise awareness and mindfulness in regard to achieving their goals (Körhasan et al., 2018). In doing so, they are more empowered in the process, leading to greater student agency.

Growing Capacity in Problem-Solving

A popular tool used in building capacity in others is often referred to as the Coaching Spectrum (Downey, 2003). This spectrum signifies how the more directive approach of problem-solving (e.g., telling, instructing, giving advice) only continues to solve someone's problems for them, whereas the non-directive approach (e.g., paraphrasing, reflecting, listening to understand) leads an individual to learn how to solve problems on their own. The spectrum also provides various other options that fall in differing levels between the two ends of the spectrum.

Without question, Bloom's (1956) Taxonomy and the Revised Bloom's Taxonomy (Anderson et al., 2014) are commonplace among many gifted classrooms. When addressing goal setting with gifted and high-potential learners, these same higher-order thinking skills should be addressed

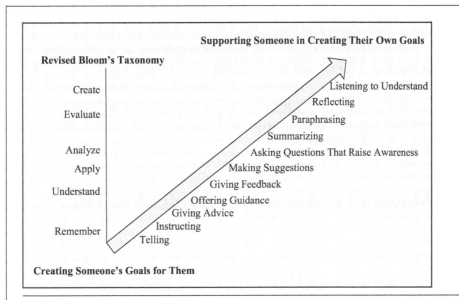

Figure 2.1 Goal Setting through the Revised Bloom's Taxonomy

Note: Adapted from Downey (2003).

(Anderson et al., 2014)

simultaneously while developing goals and creating student agency. Figure 2.1 illustrates the integration of the Coaching Spectrum and the Revised Bloom's Taxonomy and provides a visual of how higher-order thinking skills and developing student agency work in tandem to empower gifted and high-potential learners in goal development.

In taking a look at this figure, reflect back to Chapter 1 and its discussion of how frequently goals are "given" to students. In doing so, gifted and high-potential learners often do not see the value in the goal, let alone take ownership of it. This, in turn, may lead to negative outcomes. Through the practice of *telling* students their goals, teachers are subsequently asking them to work at the lower levels of the Revised Bloom's Taxonomy (2014) in the goal-setting process. In essence, when a goal is assigned, the student is being led to *remember* the goal, and there is no opportunity to take ownership in the process of goal development. Likewise, as students are given advice, guidance, and feedback in the goal-setting process, they are beginning to *understand* the process, and subsequently are able to begin to *apply* goal-setting behaviors more readily as small suggestions are provided. When students are asked questions about the goals, their awareness is heightened, and they begin to *analyze* their situations, choices, and behaviors as key aspects to developing personalized goals. Finally, as students have someone summarize, paraphrase, and reflect upon their goal-setting ideas alongside them, they begin to *evaluate* next steps, which leads to *creating* their own goals. By developing these skills over time and having a teacher who is able to listen for understanding throughout the process, skills are further strengthened. Not only does this approach continue to guide gifted and high-potential learners to think more critically about goal setting, it also continues to build student agency and create strong self-advocacy behaviors.

Moving Forward with Student Agency

The goal of this chapter was to signify the importance of creating student agency within the goal-setting and goal-attainment process. As the chapter title indicates, student agency is the driving force behind the PEGS Model. With this understanding and the foundational context of PEGS as shared in Chapter 1, the following chapters will focus more intently on the structures, protocols, and progressions of the PEGS process. Ultimately, the PEGS Model provides a context for an equitable approach to goal setting for gifted and high-potential learners. It is focused on building capacity in students, so they are empowered to not only create meaningful and purposeful goals within an educational learning space, but also to recognize and leverage their personal strengths to connect to our global world and make a difference.

References

Anderson, L. W., & Bloom, B. S. (2014). *A taxonomy for learning, teaching, and assessing: A revision of Bloom's Taxonomy of Educational Objectives.* Pearson.

Bandura, A. (1989). Perceived self-efficacy in the exercise of personal agency. *The Psychologist: Bulletin of the British Psychological Society, ?,* 411–424.

Bloom, B. S. (1956). *Taxonomy of educational objectives: The classification of educational goals by a committee of College and University Examiners.* Longmans.

Cash, R. M. (2016). *Self-regulation in the classroom: Helping students learn how to learn.* Free Spirit Press.

Clark, B. (2008). *Growing up gifted: Developing the potential of children at school and at home* (7th ed.). Pearson Prentice Hall.

Downey, M. (2003). *Effective coaching: Lessons from the coach's coach.* Cengage.

Flavell, J. H. (1979). Metacognition and cognitive monitoring: A new area of cognitive-development inquiry. *American Psychologist, 34*(10), 906–911.

Gagné, F. (2021). *Differentiating giftedness from talent: The DMGT perspective on talent development.* Routledge.

Körhasan, N. D., Eryilmaz, A., & Erkoç, S. (2018). The role of metacognition in students' mental models of the quantization. *Science Education International, 29*(3), 183–191. https://files.eric.ed.gov/fulltext/EJ1190 550.pdf

Nagaoka, J., Farrington, C. A., Ehrlich, S. B., & Heath, R. D., with Johnson, D. W., Dickson, S., Turner, A. C., Mayo, A., & Hayes, K. (2015). *Foundations for young adult success: A developmental framework.* The University of Chicago Consortium on Chicago School Research.

Poon, J. D. (2018). *Part 1: What do you mean when you say "student agency"?* Insights. https://education-reimagined.org/what-do-you-mean-when-you-say-student-agency/

Schunk, D., & Zimmerman, B. J. (2012). *Motivation and self-regulated learning: Theory, research, and application.* Routledge.

Sisk, D. (2021). Managing the emotional intensities of gifted students with mindfulness practices. *Education Sciences, 11*(731), 1–12. https://doi.org/10.3390/educsci11110731

Vaughn, M. (2018). Making sense of student agency in the early grades. *Phi Delta Kappan, 99*(7), 62–66. https://doi.org/10.1177/0031721718767864

Vygotsky, L. S. (1978). *Mind in society: The development of higher psychological processes.* Harvard University Press.

Wenger, E. (1998). *Communities of practice: Learning, meaning, and identity.* Cambridge University Press.

Wigfield, A., & Eccles, J. S. (2002). *Development of achievement motivation.* Academic Press.

CHAPTER 3

Purposeful Empowerment in Goal Setting

An Overview

Purposeful Empowerment in Goal Setting (PEGS) is an easily implemented model for student goal setting that incorporates a strength-based approach with a focus on social-emotional awareness, self-advocacy, and underachievement in gifted and high-potential learners. The PEGS Model is a research-based tool for teachers to empower gifted students to take control of their lives and education. The PEGS Model is represented by a simple flowchart (see Figure 3.1) that is easy for a student and teacher to follow and can encourage student agency through goal setting.

This chapter will discuss how PEGS can be implemented with gifted and high-potential students. Whether used within a one-on-one teacher–student model, a whole group model with teacher conferencing, or a peer-to-peer model with teacher facilitation, PEGS begins with establishing respectful interactions and understanding where students' natural abilities and strengths lie. Connections from students' natural abilities will guide the goal-setting process through intrapersonal awareness, interpersonal skills, and application to the learning process. Self-reflection, metacognition, and self-regulation will also be briefly discussed within this overview of the PEGS Model, as these are integral components to the development of student agency. This goal-setting model is designed to empower gifted and high-potential students to create purposeful and attainable goals in order to reach their potential.

DOI: 10.4324/9781003331049-4

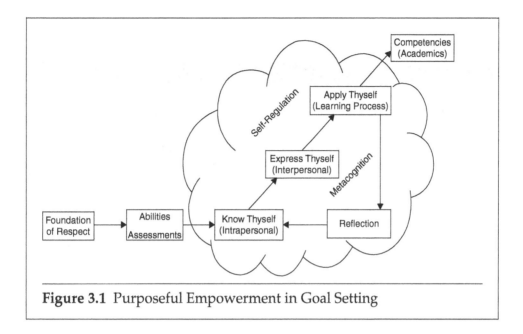

Figure 3.1 Purposeful Empowerment in Goal Setting

Founded in Respect

The PEGS Model begins with a strong foundation in respect. Gifted and high-potential students must feel heard and valued in this process. In addition, the student requires a mutually trusting and respectful relationship with the teacher, mentor, or peer in order for them to fully buy in to this goal-setting process. The teacher must first model respect for themself and for others. Modeling respect for ourselves will give students examples of how to respect themselves.

The teacher can do this by using positive self-talk, reflecting on times they have been assertive and advocated for their own needs, being honest about mistakes they have made, and modeling how to give themself grace. Respectful interactions and relationships are key for the PEGS Model to be a successful tool for student goal setting.

The teacher must also show respect for the student. In their interactions, teachers might be perceived as condescending to students. "You never turn in your homework on time." "You should be on time to class no matter what." "You should find better friends." You are always hanging out with the wrong crowd." "You…" and "You should…" statements tell students that they are inferior and incapable of problem-solving themselves. In using these types of phrases, teachers are creating a barrier in the teacher–student relationship that keeps the student from ever really buying in to what they have to say. By using a respectful alternative that

TABLE 3.1

Respectful Alternatives

"You/You Should..." Statement	Respectful Alternative Statement
You are confused because **you** goof around in class all the time.	I wonder why you feel confused. Do you have any thoughts about what is causing this?
You are so disorganized! **You** never turn in your assignments on time.	I see you haven't turned in the last two assignments. Let's problem-solve to figure out how you can get those points back.
You should put your handouts in the correct section of your binder, so it's not so messy.	It looks like you're having a little trouble keeping up with your handouts. How could you find them more easily?
You should forget about the issue with your friend and focus on your schoolwork. Middle school relationships don't matter anyway.	It sounds like the issue with your friend is really making you upset. Relationships can be tough.

is observational and validating (see Table 3.1), the student will be more likely to react positively to the change that needs to happen.

Gifted and high-potential students have their own perspectives, approaches, and strengths, and teachers must see the student as a whole person who deserves the level of respect given to a colleague. When teachers show this respect for students, more buy-in is created for this program. We are showing the student that *they* are in control of their lives, and *we* are here to support them. Also, when a teacher shows respect for the student, the student will in turn show respect for the teacher and begin to respect themselves. This foundation initiates respectful, straightforward conversations between teacher and student. The trust that comes with respect helps the student to feel the purpose behind the goals they are setting.

The PEGS Model is a shame-free zone. This authentic connection is what the student needs in order to fully invest in the goals they have set. In the book, *How To Talk So Kids Can Learn*, the authors state that respect must be given in order for students to learn to respect themselves and others (Faber et al., 1995). Once a respectful relationship is established, the focus turns to identifying the student's strengths. Table 3.2 provides suggestions for showing respect for gifted and high-potential students.

TABLE 3.2

Tips for Showing Respect for Gifted and High-Potential Students

Tips for Showing Respect for Gifted and High-Potential Students
• Avoid comparing the student to their peers or other gifted students.
• Avoid put-downs and judgmental or off-hand remarks to the student.
• Avoid sarcasm when directed at the student's person or actions.
• Avoid correcting the student publicly.
• Avoid speaking negatively about the student with teachers or parents.

Uncovering Natural Abilities

In the assessment stage of PEGS, gifted and high-potential students are given one or more inventories to find what strengths and barriers are contributing to their achievement at school, home, and in their intrapersonal awareness. Assessing a student's natural abilities, intrapersonal awareness, and interpersonal skills is a way to find their unique talents which can guide them in what they would like to target for the future. Chapter 4 provides intrapersonal and interpersonal assessments in areas such as personality, motivations, resiliency, and core values to increase student self-awareness and begin the process of goal setting.

A high level of self-awareness is extremely important in helping gifted and high-potential students see the value of setting goals. The student and the teacher analyze the assessment data and find where the student's attitudes, motivations, core values, and personality align. This information enables the goal-setting team to identify areas of talents and strengths, as well as what weaknesses might be causing problems for the student. In shedding light on these strengths and barriers, the student will find areas that need to be targeted, whether academic or otherwise. The teacher and student can then develop a short-term goal to address the need, while incorporating the student's identified strengths to lead to the desired outcome.

Highlighting Intrapersonal Awareness

In the Know Thyself stage of the PEGS Model, gifted and high-potential students explore their intrapersonal skills and knowledge. The goal-setting team (i.e., teacher and student, mentor and student) analyzes the data found in the intrapersonal and interpersonal assessments in order for the student to understand themselves as a learner. Many of the barriers that inhibit a student's ability to perform at their best in and out of school come from within themself. Thinking back to Gagné's (2021) Differentiating Model of Giftedness and Talent (DMGT) as discussed in Chapter 1, the intrapersonal component focuses on the student's temperament, personality, and resilience, as well as their self-awareness, what motivates them, and how autonomous they are (Gagné, 2021). These attributes often dictate how well a student will do in the classroom and overall in life.

In this stage of PEGS, the teacher and student will use the analysis of the assessments given to explore what makes them who they are. The student begins to recognize that what they think and feel are valid and contributing factors to their life and discovers how their feelings affect their learning. For example, a student might discover that they perform better in classes where they feel respected by the teacher, or perhaps a student might realize their interest in art provides the insight that using sketchnoting in class improves retention of learning. Students begin to see how to build confidence in themselves, what motivates them, and that their emotions are valid.

Knowing their attributes also sheds light on what barriers they have in things such as time management, work completion, autonomy, accountability, and perfectionism. The students paint themselves as a whole picture, the good and the bad, and are able to begin seeing what needs to change. Acknowledging the real self can lead to the growth that is necessary in developing a heightened sense of identity (Piechowski, 1997). To do this, the teacher will guide the student in using their strengths to find ways to overcome their barriers through goal setting. This might include asking questions such as: "If you are struggling with time management, what steps might you take to recognize what is getting in your way?" or "How can you enjoy the process of school more now that you know where your strengths lie?" Gifted and high-potential students have excellent buy-in during this step in the PEGS process because they are discussing their favorite topic—themselves! This buy-in continues as long as the teacher continues to maintain a respectful relationship with the student and becomes a guide rather than a judge. Understanding oneself is the first step to setting purposeful goals.

Understanding Interpersonal Skills

Communication is an integral component in achieving one's goals. In order for gifted and high-potential students to recognize their talents and attain the goals they set, they must advocate for themselves with teachers and parents, strengthen the bonds of the support system around them, and understand tasks that are expected of them. In the Express Thyself stage of the PEGS Model, the teacher and student will focus on the communication skills the student has strengths in and explore where their communication skills can be strengthened.

The foundation of cultivating effective speech, committed listening, and verbal and nonverbal behaviors promotes agency within the student (see Chapter 2). These skills enable gifted and high-potential students to recognize how their words and behaviors affect a situation. With effective speech, students are able to advocate for themselves in situations inside and outside of the school setting. Committed listening and appropriate verbal/nonverbal behaviors promote understanding between the student and peers, the student and teachers, and the student and parents. When they are better able to understand and communicate in a situation, the student develops agency over their consequential actions. They can then begin to strengthen their skills in problem-solving, conflict resolution, and adapting to change. Additionally, communication is key within the areas of the developmental process component of Gagné's (2021) DMGT. Skills that are recognized and strengthened within the interpersonal stage of PEGS enables the student to have ownership over the activities they pursue, the progress they make, and their investment into their future. PEGS recognizes that communication is a complex skill, but it is vital in empowering students for the future.

Applying Skills to the Learning Process

In the Apply Thyself stage of the PEGS Model, we put the gifted and high-potential students' intrapersonal and interpersonal awareness into practice. After analyzing the student's intrapersonal and interpersonal skills, the student chooses a barrier that they are struggling with at the time. An example might be failing to turn in work or feeling bored in class because they already know the material. The student and teacher then examine what intrapersonal and interpersonal strengths the student has that may aid in the situation and what skills may be contributing to the hurdle. The student and teacher then work through what type of communication should happen or other strategies that could be used to achieve the desired outcome. In the case of a student feeling bored because they already know the material, the student might decide to advocate for themself, problem-solve how to approach the teacher, and ask for more challenging material.

The PEGS Model, which guides gifted and high-potential students to set purposeful goals, also works toward a measurable outcome. Students establish the desired outcome before pursuing the goal and then reflect on what actually happened. Teacher and student can easily see if the goal has been met and how to proceed toward the next goal. The beauty of this strategy is that it is ongoing. The teacher will use this process in each session to help the student build on their goals. Students are also able to choose the goal and the method of achieving the goal, which increases student agency.

Reflection, Metacognition, and Self-Regulation

Throughout PEGS, teachers guide gifted and high-potential students to set goals through the areas of intrapersonal, interpersonal, and application to the learning process, while thinking about their thinking (i.e., metacognition) and monitoring and regulating their emotions (i.e., self-regulation). The teacher also provides the student the opportunity to reflect on the outcome of the goal. Depending on the outcome, the process begins again, either by sifting out what went wrong and trying to meet the revised goal again, or by moving on to a new goal. Through continued metacognition, self-regulation, and self-reflection, the student will be empowered to exhibit their competencies. In conjunction with the Revised Bloom's (1956, 2014) Taxonomy (see Chapter 2), the student will analyze who they are in the intrapersonal stage, evaluate what they discover about themself and how they express themself in the interpersonal component, and create an opportunity to become the person they would like to be within application to the learning process.

Goal Setting and the Gifted Student

Frequently, students set goals for themselves that are never realized. Gifted and high-potential learners may set goals that are too lofty or too simple, leaving them without the confidence that comes as a result of small wins. The threat of someone seeing that they may not be perfect and the resulting procrastination can keep the student in feelings of stress. This stress can create a situation where student goals are never achieved. As discussed in Chapter 1, gifted and high-potential students, in general, are rarely given opportunities to set their own goals within their school careers. Many times, goals are given to the student by teachers, parents, and coaches. These goals tend to be based on student deficits or skills that have not yet been mastered. Not only do these goals point out to a high-potential student that they are not perfect, they also inadvertently tell the student that they do not have the knowledge or wherewithal to know what types of goals they should set for themself. The student has no agency over what they are learning, no autonomy over skills they want to pursue, and no end-point that motivates them to where they want to be.

Reframing Goal Setting

To develop student agency, autonomy, and confidence, it is important that gifted and high-potential students be involved in the goal-setting process. Sternberg's Theory of Successful Intelligence requires the student to use their own intelligence to set and achieve goals for their life within social and cultural contexts (Sternberg, 1999). In order for the student to do this, they must identify their own strengths and weaknesses and use these to their advantage (Sousa, 2009). Within the PEGS Model, gifted and high-potential students are the conductors of the goal-setting train, with the teacher, other faculty, peers, and parents acting as the support system that prevents the train from derailing and keeps it moving forward. Students should be in charge of where they want to go and how they choose to get there. In the PEGS process, students will focus intrapersonally, getting to know themselves and their long-term plans, goals, and values. This knowledge will help them create a map for where they would like to be and how to get there. When teachers respect student opinions, ideas, and speak to them without judgment, gifted and high-potential students feel empowered to make decisions for themselves. These decisions can be focused down into small, attainable, short-term goals. Short-term and attainable goals give the student opportunities to be successful and increase motivation to pursue future goals.

Clearing the Hurdles

Once gifted and high-potential students have an idea of where they are driving the goal-setting train, it is important to decide how they will get there. As in any journey worth taking, there will be roadblocks and barriers that need to be overcome. Students may notice what the issue is and not know exactly how to clear the hurdle. The PEGS process sets the teacher and student up in a mentor–mentee relationship that supports the student in the issue. The teacher and student evaluate the situation, explore strategies and problem-solve, and develop a plan of action. The teacher and student also reflect on the outcome of the situation, giving the student clarity on what happened. The student is then empowered with tools for tackling similar situations in the future.

Goal-Setting Scenarios

Gifted and high-potential learners will encounter a myriad of different types of goals throughout their lives. They will be given and will set educational goals within their school experience. They will be given and set goals within their social and personal lives. They will set long and short-term goals for their future. They will set goals to achieve the autonomy they need in order to become contributing members of society. In the following sections, the PEGS Model will be applied to each of these goal-setting scenarios, and a brief description of its use will be covered. PEGS is versatile in its use with students and can be applied to each stage of life.

Goals within the Education Program

Whether it be goal setting with gifted and high-potential students in general, or with students who have an Individualized Education Program (IEP) or the like, goals are often annually set for these students. Best practices in goal setting state that goals must describe the intended outcome for the student, be measurable and specific to the criteria required, be realistic for the student, and have a timeline. However, as discussed in Chapter 1, a large piece of the puzzle seems to be missing from the goals set in the above plans. Gifted and high-potential students are rarely consulted about the measurable outcomes they would like to see for themselves.

When setting goals, it is important for the student to know and plan how to use their unique strengths to achieve the desired outcome. In general, when a teacher is writing a plan for a student, they use assessment data and then base the goals around the identified deficits. The PEGS Model takes a new approach in developing these goals. In the first stage of PEGS, the student explores and recognizes their strengths and the barriers to their learning. With this new self-awareness, they choose a barrier they would like to tackle, describe which of their strengths can be an asset in the situation, decide on a specific method of problem-solving to be used, and detail their intended outcome. By reframing the process in which the goals are developed, the student has ownership of the goal. The goal means something to them. It is not just an arbitrary goal given to them by someone else. The goal has a purpose for their life and their education.

If an education plan is written for a gifted or high-potential student, the teacher and student can work together to develop annual goals that best fit their focus and their values. During regular meetings or conferences with the teacher, the student can then set short-term goals that break the annual goal down into smaller, more easily attainable goals for the student to achieve. These smaller goals will not only pave the way for the student to grow within the classroom, but will also build confidence in the student as they get small, consistent wins. Confidence and a focus on their values will increase the student's motivation and create momentum leading to the next achievement. IEPs that are developed for gifted/talented and twice-exceptional learners make much more of an impact in the lives of students when they feel in control of their future.

Goals within Student Conferencing

Author James Clear (2020) suggests that goals are like the rudder on a boat, as the rudder sets the course for where you want to go. However, the rudder will not actually get you to that place. A goal may be important and a good thing to have, but it will not be realized without further action. Clear (2020) also states that systems are like the oars of the boat. The oars will propel you farther with each stroke you make. Systems that are put into place toward the goal are what propel you to the end. Students are excellent at describing what they want to do:

- ❑ "My goal is to memorize the entire periodic table."
- ❑ "I want to turn in all of my homework this semester."
- ❑ "I plan on reading one hundred books by May."
- ❑ "My goal is to bring my materials to class every day."

While each of the goals above are acceptable, the rudder alone will not get them to that outcome. Gifted and high-potential students must develop regular systems that will propel them to the finish.

During student conferences, the teacher implements the PEGS process with the student to introduce them to developing a system for achieving their goals. Purposeful Empowerment in Goal Setting is an ongoing system that is used regularly with the student to help them focus on their strengths and values, set purposeful goals, create a plan of execution, and then reflect on their progress. When the student has this tool in their toolbelt, they will have the autonomy to develop and achieve their goals into adulthood.

Goals for Future Aspirations

For many gifted and high-potential students, their lives are geared toward the future. Their intellectual and creative prowess cause parents, teachers, and even the student to think about the great things they may be able to achieve in their lives. Some students decide on what they want to do for a career or what college they would like to attend when they are in elementary school. Having lofty goals is not something to necessarily discourage, but something to tease out fully and create a plan for. Students may think that just earning good grades will lead them to achieving these goals. Making good grades is one way to achieve future goals, but there are many other skills and habits the student should develop in order to be successful in the world.

The PEGS Model as a tool for future goal setting can provide gifted and high-potential students with small successes that lead to greater accomplishments. Teachers who implement PEGS with their students provide opportunities for the students to understand who they are, what strengths they have that can lead to contributions to the world, what core values they never want to compromise, and how to communicate and problem-solve with the people around them. When thinking about the student's long-term goals, the teacher is able to aid the student in breaking the goal down into smaller, more easily attainable short-term goals that aim the student for the trajectory to success.

While in middle school, students who go through the PEGS process have a greater understanding of who they are as high-potential students. With this understanding, they begin to have more ownership of their achievements in school. At this age, students acquire the skills of setting goals, following through with the goal, and adapting to success or failure (Rakow, 2020). The PEGS process challenges them to build the skills that are needed for success in high school. High levels of motivation come when students see the small actions they are taking, leading to better grades and relationships.

High school presents its own set of challenges when it comes to a student's future aspirations. Gifted and high-potential students in high school may experience lower levels of self-confidence and higher levels of perfectionism than their peers (Souza, 2009). In fact, many high-potential students are unsure of how to plan and navigate the best course for what they would like to achieve. For example, gifted and high-potential students are generally expected to take a college route that requires Honors and Advanced Placement courses. Parents and counselors tend to encourage these students to take as many of these courses as possible, whether the student has a talent in that area or not. Intense and rigorous course loads, large amounts of homework, and other expected extracurricular activities greatly increase the student's anxiety and can possibly cause other issues such as underachievement, psychological stress, and exhaustion. With the PEGS Model, the student receives support in navigating their intense course load and builds self-regulation strategies. Having the teacher as their coach in this enables the student to build the resilience needed to tackle future challenges. The PEGS Model is also useful in supporting the student as they complete college applications, in tracking the tasks involved in applying to college, and in successfully completing rigorous coursework.

College, however, may not be in the sights of some gifted and high-potential students. The PEGS Model also supports the student in finding what jobs and other types of community involvement may lead them to the goals they envision for themselves. Local internships and other technical and career programs may fit the desires of the student better than college prep courses. Because of their work within the PEGS process, the student will be able to look at themselves with a magnifying glass in order to reveal their passions and talents.

Goals Beyond School

There is a popular saying that "adulting is hard." In her bestselling book, *How to Raise an Adult*, Julie Lythcott-Haims discusses over-parenting which has become the norm (Lythcott-Haims, 2016). According to Lythcott-Haims, parents, especially those of high-potential students, push their children toward the best classes, activities, and colleges while being their personal handler, chauffeur, chef, and assistant. The parents do everything necessary to make sure the child is checking off the boxes in order to achieve the lofty goals the parents have set. The students become burned out, lack the skills they need in order to live on their own, and may enter a career that they do not have a passion for. This can be a serious problem for gifted and high-potential students, and teachers may be guilty of over-protecting, hand-holding, and pushing the student toward things they don't want to do. Students must be involved in thinking about their futures, deciding what things fill their cup, and be allowed to make mistakes that build resilience and problem-solving skills. School may be a part of student success, but it is not the totality of what childhood and adolescence is. Students must have opportunities to build self-efficacy.

The PEGS Model provides opportunities for gifted and high-potential students to build the habits and skills they need to accomplish the things in life that matter, whether that means paying bills on time, buying groceries within their budget, or writing an excellent dissertation. Students have the opportunity to explore what their passions are and what they want for their futures. Teachers guide students through problem-solving challenges they face instead of holding their hand and telling them what action to take. Allowing students to work through these tough situations makes a deposit into their experience bank. When the student faces other challenges in the future, they will be able to draw from the experience bank to solve the problem on their own. If they have difficulty in time management or turning in work, the teacher encourages them to find ways to solve this problem using their strengths. This builds confidence and habits that will translate into managing their time within their careers, turning in college projects by the deadline, and even in paying bills by the due date. Through the PEGS process, the student is given a designated time to focus on and build these skills and a respectful guide to walk alongside them. This builds the foundation they need in order to become successful adults who are able to achieve their goals and happiness within their lives.

Proceeding with PEGS

With a steadfast foundation in respectful interactions, a teacher provides opportunities for gifted and high-potential students to set and achieve the goals they have for themselves. In order for a student to be successful at this, it is important for them to understand who they are, what they want for their lives, and how best to make it happen. With the Purposeful Empowerment in Goal Setting process, the student discovers where their natural abilities lie, explores their strengths and weaknesses, learns to communicate with necessary stakeholders, problem-solves within their goals, and applies these skills to their own learning. This process promotes agency within the student and sets the path for them to become successful and contributing members of society.

References

Bloom, B. S. (1956). *Taxonomy of educational objectives: The classification of educational goals by a committee of college and university examiners.* Longmans.

Clear, J. (2020, November 11). *Goal setting: A scientific guide to setting and achieving goals.* James Clear. https://jamesclear.com/goal-setting

Faber, A. I. I., Mazlish, E., Nyberg, L., & Anstine Templeton, R. (1995). *How to talk so kids can learn: At home and in school.* Scribner.

Gagné, F. (2021). *Differentiating giftedness from talent: The DMGT perspective on talent development.* Routledge.

Lythcott-Haims, J. (2016). *How to raise an adult: Break free of the overparenting trap and prepare your kid for success.* St. Martin's Griffin.

Piechowski, M. M. (1997). Emotional giftedness: The measure of intrapersonal intelligence. In N. Colangelo & G. A. Davis (Eds.), *Handbook of gifted education* (2nd ed., pp. 366–381). Allyn & Bacon, Incorporated.

Rakow, S. (2020). *Educating gifted students in middle school: A practical guide.* Routledge.

Sousa, D. A. (2009). *How the gifted brain learns.* Corwin.

Sternberg, R. J. (1999). The theory of successful intelligence. *Review of General Psychology, 3*(4), 292–316. https://doi.org/10.1037/1089-2680.3.4.292

CHAPTER 4

Identifying the Needs of the Student

In order for a gifted and high-potential student's talents to be recognized and utilized, they must understand who they are and what they have to share with the world. Teachers, parents, and others may be able to see the potential in students, but it is likely students may not see this for themselves. It is important for the adults in a student's life to hold up the mirror, so the students can realize the beauty and purpose they offer, the thorns that should be pruned, and the path that they should grow. It is with the knowledge of themselves that students can plot the course for which their talents are realized.

Learning about yourself is not necessarily an easy process. The student must be vulnerable and take ownership. In this stage of Purposeful Empowerment in Goal Setting (PECS), gifted and high potential students narrow the focus to specific areas of who they are as individuals. The learner then gleans knowledge that is important to completing their education and achieving the goals they decide to set. These specific areas include understanding their intellectual giftedness and creativity, social aptitudes, psychological traits, motivation, and volition. As Gagné's (2021) DMGT suggests, these aptitudes and traits work together with the developmental process in order for students to display their talents. In this chapter, specific areas of focus and their assessments for teachers to use with students will be introduced. The goal of using these assessments is

DOI: 10.4324/9781003331049-5

for students to learn more about who they are and to apply this knowledge in the goal-setting process.

Intrapersonal and Interpersonal Assessments

In the assessment stage of PEGS, the teacher provides assessments for the student to complete and then intentionally reviews the responses with the student. The areas to be assessed are included in Table 4.1. Opportunities to reflect on the data are also provided as a way for analysis to continue and for students to make meaningful connections. This data is most valuable to the student as they navigate the PEGS process and develop into the person they would like to become.

Understanding Giftedness and Creativity

One of the best topics of conversation in a GT (Gifted and Talented) class is what it means to be gifted. The answer given most often, and possibly most dreaded by teachers, is that it means they are smart. Gifted educators understand there is much more to our students than just being smart.

TABLE 4.1

Intrapersonal and Interpersonal Assessments Resources

Area of Assessment	Assessment Resource
Giftedness and Creativity	• Resource 4.1 Giftedness and Creativity Concept Attainment and Reflection • Giftedness and Creativity Attribute Sort
Social Aptitudes	• Resource 4.2 Social Aptitudes Slider Assessment and Reflection
Temperament	• Table 4.3 Four Common Temperaments Table and Reflection
Personality	• Table 4.5 Five-Factor Personality Model Table and Reflection
Resilience	• Resource 4.3 Resiliency Questionnaire
Motivation	• Resource 4.4 Core Values Checklist and Reflection
Task Valuation	• Resource 4.5 Task Valuation Inventory
Volition	• Resource 4.6 Volition Skills Checklist and Reflection
Psychosocial Skills	• Resource 4.7 Psychosocial Skills Checklist and Reflection

Teaching gifted and high-potential students is such a gift because they challenge us, have amazing ideas, ask questions that are not obvious, and add plenty of humor. They understand complex topics quickly and feel intensely about difficult situations (Clark, 2008). Gifted and high-potential students are unique. However, in the brain development stages of adolescence, we know that they desire to be part of the herd—they just want to fit in (Cockerham et al., 2021). This creates a challenge for a teacher who wants to highlight the student's differences and celebrate them.

Providing gifted and high-potential students with an opportunity to understand traits associated with intellectual giftedness and creativity is a top priority. Resource 4.1 presents a concept development (Taba et al., 1971) exercise to support students in this learning process. Directions for completing Resource 4.1 are as follows:

1. Before using this activity, the teacher should cut out each of the phrases from *The Giftedness and Creativity Attributes Sort*.
2. In Resource 4.1, the teacher asks the student to write down as many things as they can in one minute that convey what it means to be gifted and creative. Then, the student writes down as many phrases as they can about what being gifted and creative is not.
3. Once completed, the teacher talks with the student about any of the phrases they came up with.
4. The teacher then gives the student the cut-out phrases from *The Giftedness and Creativity Attributes Sort*. The student should be instructed to sort the phrases into the categories of *gifted* and *creative*. The teacher can then encourage the student to develop other categories these can be sorted into.
5. Finally, the teacher asks the student to choose six phrases that most illustrate their own giftedness. When the activity is complete, the teacher and student discuss the reflection prompts at the end of the exercise (see Table 4.2).

RESOURCE 4.1
Giftedness and Creativity

Name: _____

Examples	Non-Examples

My Top Six
1._____
2._____
3._____
4._____
5._____
6._____

Giftedness and Creativity Attributes Sort

Interest in problem-solving	Critical thinker	Sense of justice	Heightened self-awareness	Impulsive, eager, and spirited
Voracious reader	Inventive	Sensitivity or empathy for others	Emotional depth	Intense focus on passions
Large vocabulary	Keen sense of humor	Constantly questions	High expectations of self	High expectations of others
Curiosity	Independent attitude	Thinks flexibly	Independence in work and study	Perseverance in areas of importance
Diverse interests and abilities	Intuitive	Advanced moral judgment	Frustration in difficulty meeting standards	Persistent goal-directed behavior

TABLE 4.2

Reflection Prompts for *Giftedness and Creativity*

Reflection Prompts for *Giftedness and Creativity*
• What insights did you gain after seeing your Top Six traits?
• Which of the phrases can you relate to what is going on at school right now?
• Which of the phrases can you relate most to how you interact with your friends?
• Which of the phrases are not like you at all?

Understanding Social Aptitudes

Gifted and high-potential students' social aptitudes greatly affect how they perceive themselves and how they are perceived by others. The ability to observe a social situation and understand what is happening is an integral part of critical thinking and problem-solving. A person's ability to interact with ease and use tact in those interactions can play a part in their success, whether helping or hindering. Leadership skills require a person to be able to influence and persuade others. These skills are more powerful if accompanied by charisma and eloquence. Empowering students with knowledge of their talents and skills in social interactions can not only increase their self-confidence but enable them to lead our future generations. Gifted and high-potential students could be perceived as being condescending, lacking tact and eloquence, or having poor observation skills. In order for them to show their academic talents, gifted and high-potential students should have an awareness of how they interact with the world in order for them to set appropriate goals and let the gifts they have shine through.

Resource 4.2 provides a student self-assessment focused on social aptitudes. This handout shows scales for each of the social aptitudes and a brief description of what the aptitude encompasses. Students assess themselves in these areas. The teacher and student discuss the results, and the student considers and answers the reflection prompts. This exercise will allow the teacher and student to respectfully discuss the social aptitudes the student has gifts in and what might be improved on.

RESOURCE 4.2
Social Aptitudes Slider Self-Assessment

Name: _____

Directions: The left-hand side of the slider represents low and the right-hand side of the slider represents high. Place an X on the line of the slider to show where you fall for each.

Observation and Perceptiveness:
Surveying carefully to gain understanding and having keen insight or outstanding judgment

Low   High

Social Interaction and Tact:
Action/reaction using social norms and communicating with thoughtfulness/sensitivity

Low   High

Influencing and Persuasion:
Having the ability to affect someone's thoughts and the power to convince

Low   High

Leadership and Charisma:
Having the ability to motivate a group toward a goal with enthusiasm and charm

Low   High

Social Aptitudes Reflection Prompts
• In looking at where you ranked yourself on the sliders, which areas of social aptitudes do you feel best about? Do you think you are gifted in this area?
• Which slider reveals most about who you are as a person?
• Which slider has the most influence on your life right now?
• Which slider has the potential to affect your life in the future the most?

Understanding Psychological Traits

Malcolm X said, "All of our experiences fuse into our personality. Everything that ever happened to us is an ingredient" (Malcolm X. & Haley, 1999, p. 153). Our personalities have the power to attract people and also to hide our true selves. Personality is the mixture of our important experiences, thoughts, feelings, defense mechanisms, trauma, kindnesses, and the internal way we make sense of the world. Personality then, in turn, governs how we think, act, and react in every aspect of our lives. Therefore, understanding our personality is extremely important in our journey to self-awareness.

Achieving self-awareness allows a person to observe and regulate their thoughts, feelings, and actions, promoting positive social interactions and increasing the likelihood of success in leadership and achieving goals. In order for a teacher to encourage this self-awareness, gifted and high-potential students should be provided with opportunities that allow them to reflect on their own personalities, temperament, and resilience. As students grow in self-awareness, it further empowers them to find ways to self-regulate and take control of their education and lives. The following sections provide a few activities we suggest to help the teacher start the conversation of self-awareness. These will allow the student to explore who they are and where their strengths and barriers lie.

Temperament

Think back to your college days. You walk into class to find a pop quiz over a topic that was barely covered and you did not fully understand. How would you have reacted? Would you get upset with the professor since this was not something that was on the syllabus and begin calculating how this might affect your grade? Would you have been a little frustrated with the change in routine but quickly accept it and move on? Would you make a joke to your friends about hoping you have superpowers and enthusiastically turn in the completed quiz? Or would you request the professor only use this quiz as extra credit since it was not on the syllabus and complete the quiz with as much detail and information as possible?

How we react in situations is considered our temperament. Just like in puppies, we are born with a temperament that may only change slightly over time. Temperament is considered to be biologically based and may be influenced by the person's environment (Buss & Plomin, 2014). Understanding a person's temperament can help us predict how they might approach a problematic situation or setback, how they work with others, and even how they reach their goals.

There are four commonly recognized temperament types. These types can give students a label for how they interact with the world around them. A person can be a combination of types, usually having a primary type and a secondary type. Exploring their temperament, along with personality type and resilience, will prompt the student to become more self-aware and more intentional in their lives. Teachers can use the Four Common Temperaments (see Table 4.3) to prompt gifted and high-potential students in exploring where their temperament might lie. Have the students decide which temperament may be their primary and which would be their secondary temperament. Use the Temperament Reflection Prompts (see Table 4.4) as a guide for continuing this conversation.

TABLE 4.3

Four Common Temperaments

Extroverted	Introverted
Sanguine People-oriented, outgoing, helpful, playful, impulsive, active, optimistic, good sense of humor, easily amused, affectionate	**Phlegmatic** Service-oriented, can work with others, passive, low ambition, easy-going, calm, indecisive, agreeable, patient, likes routines, resists change
Choleric Results-driven, likes goal setting, achiever, positive demeanor, self-confident, independent, quick mind, assertive, direct, opinionated, decisive, creative	**Melancholy** Detail/quality-oriented, cautious, perfectionist, rule follower, tentative in new situations, private, factual, logical, analytical, enjoys following a plan

TABLE 4.4

Reflection Prompts for *Temperament*

Reflection Prompts for *Temperament*
• In exploring your primary and secondary temperaments, how could these have played a role in an interaction you have had this week?
• Discuss ways that your temperament may not mesh well with someone else's in your life.
• Which of the attributes in your primary temperament can be considered positive, and which can be considered negative? Can you take an opposite view on these attributes?

TABLE 4.5

Five-Factor Personality Model

High Levels	Personality Factor	Low Levels
Careful, disciplined, organized, hard-working, dependable	**Conscientiousness**	Impulsive, disorganized, careless, scattered
Likable, helpful, trusting, empathetic	**Agreeableness**	Uncooperative, critical, harsh, suspicious
Has negative or difficult emotions, anxious, insecure	**Neuroticism**	Calm, emotionally stable, secure, even-keeled
Curious, imaginative, explores many interests	**Openness**	Prefers routine, practical, conforming, conventional
Outgoing, warm, seeks adventure, sociable	**Extroversion**	Quiet, withdrawn, seeks solitude, reserved, restrained

Personality

In order to better understand the student's personality, the teacher and student can explore the Five-Factor Model of Personality. This model organizes personality traits into five different areas: Extraversion, Agreeableness, Conscientiousness, Neuroticism, and Openness to Experience (Costa & McCrae, 1992). This model is widely used and easily accessible by an internet search. Using this model seen in Table 4.5, gifted and high-potential learners gain insight into how they approach situations, how they react in their social settings, and how their general actions and feelings may be governed by their personality. This also provides the student with a more global perspective in realizing that everyone does not think, feel, act, or react in the same manner they do. This knowledge will help foster the social relationships they seek.

After the Five-Factor Model has been used and personality traits are determined, the teacher and student begin analyzing these traits to identify specific strengths and areas for growth. Table 4.6 provides prompts for reflection on the student's personality traits. Self-awareness in these areas allows the student to step back from a situation they are in and see how their personality traits, strengths, and weaknesses play out in real life.

TABLE 4.6

Reflection Prompts for *Five-Factor Personality Model*

Reflection Prompts for *Five-Factor Personality Model*
• Looking at the Five Factor Personality Model, decide where you fall within each of the five factors of conscientiousness, agreeableness, neuroticism, openness, and extroversion.
• Which of the Five Factors of Personality would you say relates most to your strengths? Explain and give examples.
• Which of the Five Factors of Personality do you think create the most barriers in your life? Explain and give examples.
• Reflect on a moment or situation from this week where an aspect of your personality has been a factor. This could have been at school, with parents, or in a social situation. Explain what happened and examine if this caused a barrier or used a strength of yours.

Resilience

The American Psychological Association (2020) defines resilience as "the process of adapting well in the face of adversity, trauma, tragedy, threats, or significant sources of stress." Resilience is a person's ability to stand back up after being knocked down. It is also the process of finding a different path if the one a person is walking down is blocked. Can you swerve or pivot when things do not go as planned? Can you find a different way to complete the task when your initial method has failed? When life throws you a curveball, can you still get on base, or do you strike out? The amount of resilience someone has is based on how they act in tough situations.

Adversity, trauma, threats, and sources of stress can produce a feeling of fear in all students. While fear was an essential part of human existence in order to keep a human alive, the fear students experience daily is usually not life-threatening. A student's brain experiences this and has a similar reaction to the emotion as if they were being chased by a lion. The fear response happens in the brain's amygdala, which controls the fight, flight, or freeze reaction (Kozlowska et al., 2015), and the student cannot make appropriate decisions when this reaction is happening. Threats as small as receiving a poor grade on a piece of homework can cause this reaction and result in procrastination, arguments, and underachievement.

A student is said to be resilient if they can cope with adversity, recover from it quickly, and bounce back into action (Ford & Patry, 2016). Resiliency can be a character trait that the student already possesses, or it can be something that is developed over time. With each small success after a tough situation or seeing that they are ok after that zero on homework, the student's brain begins to realize that these things can be overcome and are a much smaller threat than once believed. When gifted and high-potential students find out more about their level of resiliency, it brings to light what they have previously been able to accomplish, builds their confidence in achieving goals, both large and small, and empowers them to take control of their lives.

In order for the student to become aware of their resiliency, the teacher can have the student complete the Resiliency Questionnaire (see Resource 4.3). This questionnaire assesses the student's self-perception of their abilities to adapt to changes, emotionally self-regulate, make decisions, persist in challenges, and gauges their level of confidence and self-talk. Results from the questionnaire give the student a window into how they bounce back from adversity and prompt them to find areas they would like to improve. It is important for the student to note which questionnaire statements describe them well and which statements do not and discuss these with the teacher. The teacher should ask the student to give examples of situations where they felt they recovered well from a stressful situation and examples of when they did not feel resilient.

RESOURCE 4.3
Resiliency Questionnaire

Name: _____

Directions: After each prompt, put a minus (-) in the box if the statement does not describe you and a plus (+) in the box if the statement describes you.

Resiliency Prompt	+ or -
I am self-confident and know who I am.	
I use positive self-talk and believe in myself.	
I am kind to myself and focus on my own self-care.	
In a tough situation, I can calm myself down and focus on what I should do.	
I can reflect on my experiences and learn from them.	
I can recover emotionally from setbacks and problems.	
I am durable in tough times.	
I adapt quickly to changes and bounce back from difficulties.	
I base my decisions on what I can and cannot control.	
Difficult experiences make me stronger and a better person.	
I am mostly optimistic and know I can overcome challenges.	
I reframe bad luck into opportunities and see the benefits.	
I can keep on going despite difficulties.	

Reflection: How do the above statements impact your ability to bounce back from adversity?

Motivation

As the teacher continues to hold up the mirror to the student, it is important for the student to see what motivates them. Motivation is the force that drives and pushes a person toward a goal. Many times, motivations are not evident. When comparing two gifted students in the same grade, one student may be underachieving, acting out, and finding ways to avoid challenges alongside a student who is quiet, respectful, and driven to have the top grade in the class. Understanding why their behaviors are so different, even though they both have exceptional intellect, comes down to who they are and where their motivation lies. The underachieving student may have parents who continuously put pressure on them to change their actions which, in turn, motivates the student to avoid work and retreat to things that give them pleasure in life, like a favorite video game. The high achiever may be motivated by praise or by the end goal of having a happy life because they want to have a stable career and comfortable income as an adult. Sifting out their motivation can be a useful tool for students as they are looking to set goals that allow them to exhibit their gifts and talents.

To explore a student's motivation, a teacher can lead the student in conversations about their values, interests, and passions. In general, adolescents rarely know what their core values are. They may have experience with values from a church or from lessons taught by their parents. However, the student probably has not given much thought to what they value most in their life. Using Resource 4.4, the teacher prompts the student to explore the list of core values, evaluates which ones are the most relevant to their life, and circles their top eight values. When finished, the teacher asks the student what they think their top three values are and has them explain why they feel this way. Students then complete the 3-2-1 Values Reflection. The Core Values Reflection Prompts (see Table 4.7) continue to guide conversations.

RESOURCE 4.4
"Know Thyself" Core Values

Name: _____

3-2-1 Reflection

Describe three things that give you the most joy: _____

Describe two things that you would like to achieve: _____

Describe one thing that motivates you to take action: _____

Core Values List – Circle Your Top 8.

Family	Wisdom	Leadership
Freedom	Beauty	Contentment
Security	Caring	Health
Loyalty	Personal Development	Courage
Intelligence	Honesty	Balance
Connection	Adventure	Compassion
Creativity	Kindness	Fitness
Humanity	Teamwork	Professionalism
Success	Communication	Relationship
Respect	Learning	Knowledge
Invention	Excellence	Patience
Diversity	Innovation	Prosperity
Generosity	Commonality	Wellness
Integrity	Contributing	Gratitude
Love	Spiritualism	Grace
Openness	Strength	Endurance
Religion	Entertainment	Effectiveness
Order	Wealth	Fame
Joy/Play	Power	Justice
Forgiveness	Affection	Trusting Your Gut
Work Smarter Not Harder	Cooperation	Forgiveness
Excitement	Friendship	Self-Respect
Change	Relationships	Abundance
Goodness	Encouragement	Enjoyment
Involvement	Pride in Your Work	Entrepreneurial
Faith	Clarity	Happiness
	Charisma	Harmony
	Humor	Peace

TABLE 4.7

Reflection Prompts for *"Know Thyself" Core Values*

Reflection Prompts for *"Know Thyself" Core Values*
• After ranking your top core values, what is one realization you had or something you discovered about yourself? • Discuss a core value you have that surprised you or one that you feel should be on your list and is not. • How do your core values impact your daily actions? Your future goals? • Do your motivations impact your daily life or your future more? Explain. • How can you align your motivation, passion, values, and goals?

Task Valuation

Student motivation is often directly related to how the student values the task. In considering Expectancy-Value Theory, a student places value on a task or outcome, determines their probability of success in that task, and this decides the amount of effort the student will give to the task (Wigfield & Eccles, 2002). In this formula, a student's expectations of themself, the attractiveness of the task or goal, and if they can attain the goal either motivates them or discourages them from attempting the goal. Because each student has distinct abilities, self-esteem, and self-regulation strategies, the student's achievement and how they perceive that achievement will differ from their peers. A student's achievement values can be looked at in four distinct ways: intrinsic value, attainment value, utility value, and cost (Vahidi, 2015; Wigfield & Eccles, 2002). When the student is armed with knowledge of how they value certain tasks, they will be able to determine how to increase their motivation when it wanes.

Intrinsic Value

Intrinsic value is a motivation from within to do well (Vahidi, 2015; Wigfield & Eccles, 2002). Gifted and high-potential students are often intrinsically motivated to do well on a task they enjoy, one that is exciting or thought-provoking, or new and appropriately challenging. Lacking intrinsic value may result in a student producing sub-par work, giving up on assignments, and in possible underachievement. Students typically lose the intrinsic value of a task whenever it is too challenging or not challenging enough, uninteresting or redundant, and has no personal relevance for the student. Intrinsic value can be extremely impactful in student achievement, as it directly relates to the student's inner world and their personal interests.

Attainment Value

A student's attainment value also relates to their inner world, especially their inner perception of who they are. In attainment value, a student's achievements come as a vote for the identity they have for themself (Vahidi, 2015; Wigfield & Eccles, 2002). For instance, a student who considers themself to be a good gymnast will work to achieve each skill and build to harder skills. Gifted and high-potential students may see themselves as intelligent and set goals for themselves based on this belief. However, this may look different according to each student. They may set goals based on overall academic achievements, on one type of course or subject, or on intellectual pursuits outside of school. Because this type of value is based on the student's perception of themself, it is important for the student to have a good understanding of who they are and a realistic perception of their potential.

Utility Value

A high-achieving student may be solely motivated by the future goals a task relates to. This is considered utility value, the value a task has because it is utilized to achieve future goals (Vahidi, 2015; Wigfield & Eccles, 2002). Students may value daily schoolwork very little but always do well on it because they are motivated by it leading to college opportunities. Utility value can also be leveraged when students recognize how learning connects with their future career aspirations or how it might contribute to a comfortable lifestyle in their future where they are able to satisfy their wants and needs and have the freedom to make those decisions (Phelps, 2022). Through understanding this type of valuation and goal setting, a student may even be able to reverse underachievement (Emerick, 1992).

Cost

While the way a student values a task can lead to increased motivation, the cost of completing the task may counteract the motivating effect. When a student is presented with a task, they consider what amount of effort needs to be given to the task, what the task will mean emotionally, and what other activities they will not be able to give their time to because of the task (Vahidi, 2015; Wigfield & Eccles, 2002). This is the cost of them completing the task. If they perceive the cost to be too high, the task will either not be completed or will be postponed to another time, thus possibly contributing to underachievement.

Gifted and high-potential students can easily spot tasks that are worth the cost and the ones that are not. In the adolescent years when social perceptions are in the forefront of students' minds, how they may be perceived socially after completing a task might have the heftiest cost. Even a task as simple as completing homework may have a high cost for a student if they are exhausted from a day of rigorous classes and extracurriculars or would like to use the time for down-time pursuits, such as hobbies or video games.

Using the Task Valuation Inventory (see Resource 4.5), the gifted student is prompted to reflect on how they perform in class and at home, what things are most interesting to them, what they value and are proud of, and what they would like to accomplish in the future. After completing this inventory, the teacher and student should discuss the student's responses. During this discussion, the teacher should highlight what the student finds to be intrinsically valuable, what beliefs about themselves are motivational, what future goals they are working toward, and what tasks cost the most for the student to complete. The student should have some realizations that can propel them toward setting goals that mean the most to them or have the most impact on their future.

RESOURCE 4.5
Task Valuation Inventory

Name: _____

Directions: Please complete all of the following sentences as they relate to your school career. There are no right or wrong answers. Write the first thing that comes into your mind.

1. When I try hard at school, it's because _____
_____

2. I would spend more time on my schoolwork if _____
_____

3. If I do poorly in school, then _____
_____

4. When I don't try hard in school, it is because _____
_____

5. Doing well in school will help me to _____
_____

6. School is important because_ _____
_____

7. The thing I am most interested in learning more about is _____
_____

8. The most interesting thing I have learned this year is _____
_____

9. I feel best about myself when _____
_____

10. I feel worst about myself when _____
_____

11. I am most proud of _____
_____

12. I wish that I could _____

_____

13. When I grow up, I want to _____

_____

14. I really value _____

_____

15. I don't want to give up _____

_____

Reflection Directions: After you have completed the sentences, discuss your answers with your teacher. Pay close attention to finding what motivates you from within, beliefs about yourself, future goals you have for yourself, and what it costs to complete school tasks.

Things that motivate me:	Things that I believe about myself:
Future goals I have:	Cost of completing schoolwork:

Note: Adapted from Vahidi (2015).

Volition

The next area of identification for the student is one focused mainly on tasks. Tasks and goals are set for students regularly at school, at home, and in their extracurricular activities. They set goals and tasks for themselves, as well. Some gifted and high-potential students may have social-emotional barriers that inhibit their ability to complete tasks. Others may be highly talented in this area. Assessing a student's volition can provide great insight into their inner dialogue and how they will complete tasks and achieve goals in the future. Volition can be thought of as following through with a task in the face of distractions and other outside challenges or the passion of working toward a goal (Gagné, 2021; Keller, 2020). Writer's block is a great example of an outside challenge. Volitional competence would enable the writer to remember the last time they experienced writer's block and how they were able to overcome it instead of giving in to it and quitting the assignment. There are a few contributors to a person's volition, namely planning the task, planning for roadblocks, regulation of emotions, and strategies for increasing motivation and effort. When a student understands which parts of this process enable performance and which parts are erecting barriers, they will be able to employ strategies that increase their volition and empower themself to use their talents.

In an effort to find where their volition lies, teachers can explore this with students using the Volition Skills Checklist (see Resource 4.6). Using this checklist, students choose which statements best represent them for each of the prompts. A tally of the checkmarks will reveal the strengths and barriers the student is showing in their volition. The teacher and student should then discuss ways in which the student's volition affects them in the classroom, completing work at home, and in their extracurriculars. The teacher can also speak with the student about any strategies they have used in the past that increased their volition.

RESOURCE 4.6
Volition Skills Checklist

Name: _____

Directions: Place a checkmark in the column that best describes your actions when working on tasks.

	Very much like me	Some-what like me	Neutral	Not like me	Not at all like me
I set goals for my learning.					
I am always prepared to work hard in class.					
I plan my tasks to achieve my goals.					
I have a strong commitment to achieving my goals.					
When I lose focus, I increase my effort.					
I can set up my environment to reduce distractions.					
I can control my emotions while working on a task.					
I can avoid distractions during a task.					
I can increase my motivation when it wanes.					
Totals					

Reflection: Which skills are most like you and which are not like you? How do these affect your performance in academics, at home, and in your extra-curricular activities?

Psychosocial Skills

When working with gifted and high-potential students, teachers often comment about gifted students' inability to be organized, follow through on assignments, take leadership roles in the classroom, or manage their time wisely. While there are many gifted and high-potential students who have strengths in these areas, some students require extra support. They may not be able to control their impulses to shout out in the classroom, or they may never say a word. Emotional regulation can also pose a problem for these students. Because of their potential for asynchronous development, gifted students may have not developed the appropriate executive functioning and psychosocial skills their typical peers have. These gaps can make an extremely bright student look like they are not living up to their potential because there are so many zeros in the gradebook.

Typically, gifted and high-potential students do not understand where the gaps lie. They think they can remember all of their tasks, or they think they are contributing well to the class when they shout out the correct answers constantly. However, the gaps are evident to the teacher. In order for any progress to be made in these areas, it is important for the student to recognize where the barriers lie in the psychosocial arena.

In order to assess this area, the teacher can have the student complete the simple Psychosocial Skills Checklist (Resource 4.7). The student should be directed to read each prompt with the pronoun "I" in front of it. Then, they decide if the prompt describes what they do most of the time, sometimes, or rarely, and place a checkmark in the corresponding column. The student and teacher will use this information to complete the reflection questions (see Table 4.8).

RESOURCE 4.7
Psychosocial Skills Checklist

Name: _____

Directions: Read each prompt with the pronoun "I" in front of it. Decide if that describes what you do most of the time, sometimes, or rarely. Place a checkmark in the corresponding column.

Student:	Most of the time	Sometimes	Rarely
Feel confident and part of a group			
Express myself clearly			
Can speak in front of a group			
Show respect physically and verbally			
Express feelings, fears, and wishes			
Can handle strong emotions when around others			
Know how to calm down from strong emotions			
Am open to new activities and experiences			
Adapt to changes in routine or plans			
Can work in a group for a common goal			
Help others in the group			
Express disagreement in a non-violent way			
Can accept compromise in an argument			

Student:	Most of the time	Sometimes	Rarely
Can be actively involved when interested			
Complete assigned tasks			
Persevere when the task is difficult			
Can easily remember my commitments			
Seldom need reminders to complete tasks			
Seldom leave tasks to the last minute			
Stay focused on work			
Work until task is completed			
Resume task easily when interrupted			
Plan and complete priority tasks			
Focus on the most important tasks			
Break big tasks down into subtasks and timelines			
Am an organized person			
Keep my work area neat and organized			
Maintain systems for organizing my work			

TABLE 4.8
Reflection Prompts for *Psychosocial Checklist*

Reflection Prompts for *Psychosocial Checklist*
• According to the checkmarks in the "most of the time" column, which are your biggest strengths? How do they help you at school?   • According to the "rarely" column, what are some barriers to your school day?   • Which skill is the most significant roadblock to you showing your talents?

Benefits of Identifying Student Needs

In the assessment stage of PEGS, the teacher and student will be actively collecting data on what makes the student who they are. With the knowledge gained of the student's intellect and creativity, social skills, personality traits, resilience, motivation, volition, and psychosocial skills, the teacher and student begin to identify where barriers lie, especially in the areas of intrapersonal and interpersonal needs. If the student is exhibiting self-destructive behaviors, talking about self-harm, showing signs of severe depression, or other warning signs, it is important to refer the student to a mental health professional and follow other protocols as necessary. However, if the student's needs can be addressed at school, the social-emotional benefits will be great. Addressing and providing strategies in these areas is something that is typically missing from academic curricula and gifted interventions. Using the PEGS Model and having one-on-one and respectful conversations with the student, creating a safe place to discuss the tough issues, and providing appropriate feedback and strategies will benefit the student in immediate, everyday life, as well as in the future.

References

American Psychological Association. (2020, February 1). *Building your resilience*. American Psychological Association. www.apa.org/topics/resilience

Buss, A. H., & Plomin, R. (2014). *Temperament (PLE: Emotion): Early developing personality traits*. Psychology Press.

Clark, B. (2008). *Growing up gifted: Developing the potential of children at school and at home* (7th ed.). Pearson Prentice Hall.

Cockerham, D., Lin, L., Ndolo, S., & Schwartz, M. (2021). Voices of the students: Adolescent well-being and social interactions during the emergent shift to online learning environments. *Education and Information Technologies, 26*, 7523–7541. https://doi.org/10.1007/s10 639-021-10601-4

Costa, P. T., & McCrae, R. R. (1992). The five-factor model of personality and its relevance to personality disorders. *Journal of Personality Disorders, 6*(4), 343–359. https://doi.org/10.1521/pedi.1992.6.4.343

Emerick, L. J. (1992). Academic underachievement among the gifted: Students' perceptions of factors that reverse the pattern. *Gifted Child Quarterly, 36*(3), 140–146. https://doi.or g/10.1177/0016986 29203600304

Gagné, F. (2021). *Differentiating giftedness from talent: The DMGT perspective on talent development.* Routledge.

Keller, J. M. (2020). Development and validation of a scale to measure volition for learning. *Open Praxis, 12*(2), 161–174.

Kozlowska, K., Walker, P., McLean, L., & Carrive, P. (2015). Fear and the defense cascade: Clinical implications and management. *Harvard Review of Psychiatry, 23*(4), 263–287. https://doi.org/10.1097/HRP.0000000000000065

Malcolm X., & Haley, A. (1999). *The autobiography of Malcolm X.* Ballantine Books.

Patry, D., & Ford, R. (2016). *Measuring resilience as an education outcome.* Higher Education Quality Council of Ontario.

Phelps, V. (2022). Motivating gifted adolescents through the power of PIE: Preparedness, innovation, and effort. *Roeper Review, 44*(1), 35–48. https://doi.10.1080/02783193.2021.2005204

Taba, H., Durkin, M. C., Fraenkel, J. R., & NcNaughton, A. H. (1971). *A teacher's handbook to elementary social studies: An inductive approach* (2nd ed.). Addison-Wesley.

Vahidi, S. (2015, July 2). *Research: The National Research Center on the gifted and talented (1990–2013).* https://nrcgt.uconn.edu/underachievemen t_study/goal-valuation/gv_goalva01/

Wigfield, A., & Eccles, J. S. (2000). Expectancy–value theory of achievement motivation. *Contemporary Educational Psychology, 25*(1), 68–81. https://doi.org/10.1006/ceps.1999.1015

CHAPTER 5

Know Thyself

The First Stage of Goal Development

In the classroom, it is often difficult to see what is going on with gifted or high-potential students. Our students may easily hide their emotions and feelings beneath the mask of perfection. They may work to fit in with their peers even though they have nothing in common with them. A gifted student may have low self-esteem due to the fact that they do not know what is expected of them in social situations. They may use underachievement to veil their abilities in order to protect themselves from the jeering of their peers or pressure from their parents. One of your gifted students may be having intense feelings about a social situation or current event they have seen in the news.

When taking a look at Gagné's (2021) Differentiating Model of Giftedness and Talent (DMGT), the area of intrapersonal awareness is highlighted in two areas: physical and mental traits and contributors to goal management. Along with the student's environment, these areas greatly influence a student's developmental process and their ability to exhibit talents. The goal of the PEGS Model is to increase student agency and student autonomy by strengthening their intrapersonal awareness. This intrapersonal awareness allows the student to set up situations where they are more likely to achieve their goals, have better relationships, and live more fulfilling lives because they will truly know who they are.

DOI: 10.4324/9781003331049-6

Understanding Intrapersonal Awareness

Intrapersonal development is important for gifted and high-potential students to embark on as they prepare for adulthood. Development in this area fosters a student's ability to make decisions. Students are faced with many decisions over the course of their elementary, middle, and high school careers. During this time, an adolescent's prefrontal cortex, the area in charge of decision-making, is not fully formed, so students will many times make decisions based on emotion or gut reaction. Whether it is choosing what to reply to a friend in a text or when to begin working on a school project, developing intrapersonal awareness can help the student make the decision based on more than just impulse.

Intrapersonal development also assists gifted and high-potential students in coping with internal and external stressors. When students truly know themselves, they can note their feelings, regulate the emotion, and then be able to find a solution to the situation. Coping with feelings of inadequacy or imposter syndrome, feelings that they are not as competent as they are perceived to be, can be recognized and dealt with immediately. The ability to readily cope with these feelings can increase a student's resilience and grit in a time of challenge.

Gifted students may feel anxious or stressed when faced with situations in which they need to communicate with others. Understanding what causes the stress and how to manage it in a social situation will increase a student's self-advocacy and self-esteem. Feeling heard and validated is usually what the student is wanting in an interaction, especially with an authority figure. The fear of communication will dissipate when the student understands the fear within them and how to manage this emotion.

Through intrapersonal development, students are able to recognize and adequately use their support systems. Students may feel like they have no support system in place and retreat inward. When the student develops more intrapersonal awareness, they will be aware of established supports that are available. They will be able to recognize the positive peers and other role models in their lives that they can turn to. Students will not feel alone in this journey.

Effects of Increased Intrapersonal Awareness

Through the PEGS Model, gifted and high-potential students have an opportunity to take a deep-dive into who they are. Students are given a variety of inventories in order to pin-point their specific attributes, qualities, values, strengths and weaknesses, and attitudes and motivations. Using the data obtained from these, the student explores barriers they are facing in life. With this increased understanding, the student is able to identify and manage their feelings, problem-solve through situations, increase agency and autonomy, achieve their goals, and accept who they are as a gifted person.

There are many positive effects of developing strong intrapersonal skills. Students who have these skills have a firm understanding of who they are and what things they will not compromise on. They are confident in who they are and what they can do. They know what their motivators are and can think through their strengths and weaknesses. Students with increased intrapersonal awareness tend to be more flexible in their thinking, allowing for more thoughtful problem-solving and the resilience to pivot when things get tricky. Intrapersonal awareness also allows students to better focus their thinking, create meaningful goals, and analyze situations with a clear lens. Intrapersonal awareness increases students' likelihood of having a growth mindset and to persevere in tough situations. These skills are the foundation for problem-solving, self-advocacy, and self-efficacy.

Connection to Self-Advocacy

Each school district, school, and classroom are different, no matter the policies put into place. Gifted and high-potential students are expected to learn alongside their peers. In these settings, gifted students generally have needs that are unique and different from other students (Zedan & Bitar, 2017). Because their learning needs tend not to follow the general curriculum and teaching strategies, gifted and high-potential students have an increased need for self-advocacy. The National Center for Learning Disabilities defines self-advocacy as "a set of skills based on self-knowledge, including awareness of personal strengths and limitations, knowledge of one's rights and the ability to communicate this understanding" (Parsi et al., 2018). Advocating for oneself is essential at school, home, and in the workplace. Students must be able to communicate their needs, challenges, and strengths as these relate to their classrooms and school work. Before a student is able to communicate their needs, however, they must know what they are.

In this stage of the PEGS Model, the student will have already completed personal assessments that reveal their personality, strengths and weaknesses, core values, resilience, and motivation (see Chapter 4). The student will have a clear understanding of who they are. As in the definition given, the student will have gleaned the self-knowledge and personal awareness they need to understand where and why they may need to self-advocate.

Documenting Intrapersonal Skills

After completing the assessments and inventories available in Chapter 4, significant information about the student will be known. It is then important to make sense of this information and have discussions with the student about how the assessed attributes relate to their lives. The student may have information about themself in the areas of intellect, creativity, social skills, leadership qualities, personality, temperament, resilience, core values, task valuation, volition, and psychosocial skills. As the student and teacher sift through this personal data, they can use the Assessments Analysis (see Resource 5.1) to create a log of the student's strengths, barriers, personality traits, core values, attitudes, and motivations. This resource is an easy way for the student to see how each of these components fit together to make up their life. It is the puzzle that reveals who they really are and who they can be in the future.

Gifted and high-potential students' personality traits, core values, attitudes, and motivation serve as the students' foundation. These are the characteristics on which their actions, decisions, and future goals are built. Just like a building's foundation is what it is built on and supported by, the student's strengths and barriers are built on their inner foundation. The student's strengths come from or are made greater by these areas. Their barriers are also products of these foundational components. A student's personality traits may set them on a path to enjoy learning, but their attitude toward school may corrupt their natural curiosities. The student's core values may lead them to not compromise on their beliefs, but their motivation to be a part of the crowd may have them making decisions that do not align. Students must have opportunities to explore these areas and make connections from themselves to what occurs in their lives. The Assessments Analysis serves as a log that the teacher and student refer to in each session when analyzing a barrier or setting a new goal.

RESOURCE 5.1
Assessments Analysis

Name: _____

Strengths	Barriers

My Foundation

Personality Traits	Core Values	Attitudes	Motivation

TABLE 5.1

Intrapersonal Resources

Intrapersonal Skills Focus	Resources within the Chapter
Social Aptitudes	• Table 5.2 Social Aptitudes • Observation and Perceptiveness Activities • Leadership Skills Activities
Motivation and Values	• Resource 5.2 Most Valuable Purchase
Personality Traits	• Table 5.3 Strengthening Intrapersonal Skills Through Personality • Table 5.4 Additional Strategies for High Anxiety
Resilience	• Resource 5.3 My Focus of Control • Resource 5.4 Resiliency Strategy
Volition	• Resource 5.5 Task Planning Guide
Task Valuation	• Resource 5.6 Task Valuation Decision Tree • Resource 5.7 Task Valuation Hexagonal Thinking Activity
Psychosocial Skills	• Table 5.5 Strategies for Building Psychosocial Skills
Inner Dialogue/Mindset	• Resource 5.8 The Power of the Mind
Growth Mindset	• Resource 5.9 Growing the Mind

Increasing Intrapersonal Awareness

In the following section, interventions for strengthening intrapersonal skills are discussed. With each intrapersonal skill, potential lesson ideas are shared and corresponding resources follow. These interventions can be done within a one-on-one consulting-type setting or with a whole group of gifted and high-potential students. The intrapersonal skills covered in this section relate to the assessments presented in Chapter 4. A list of these skills is provided in Table 5.1.

Social Aptitudes

General social skills are expected to develop and increase during the middle grades (Bandura, 1986). However, gifted and high-potential students can sometimes be labeled as "socially awkward." Parents and teachers may focus solely on the student's difficulty in relating to their peers. This is possibly due to the student's asynchronous development.

Because their quickly developing intellect has surpassed their social aptitudes, they may look like they are struggling to relate to their peers. Many times, gifted and high-potential students would rather spend time with and talk to adults. Other times, students only prefer friends who share their same ideas, interests, and hobbies. Having these types of preferences for peers is not a problem. However, the student must understand how to relate to others in different types of situations. The student must be able to effectively communicate with teachers about assignments and lessons. They must work appropriately with partners in group work. They must also learn to convey their ideas in thoughtful, tactful, and respectful ways as they traverse life. Students must have skills in the areas of observation and perceptiveness, social interaction and tact, influencing and persuading others, and leadership and charisma (see Table 5.2). Strengthening peer–peer relationships and teacher–student relationships is an important step in overall social skills development (Sørlie, 2020).

While pieces of the social aptitude puzzle go with interpersonal communication, aspects including observation and perceptiveness and leadership skills begin with a student's intrapersonal awareness. Social interactions will be covered more in Chapter 6: Express Thyself.

TABLE 5.2

Social Aptitudes

Observation and Perceptiveness:	• Surveying carefully to gain understanding • Having keen insight • Having outstanding judgment in the situation
Social Interaction and Tact:	• Using social norms as a guide for action and reaction to others • Communicating with thoughtfulness and sensitivity
Influencing and Persuasion:	• Having the ability to affect someone's thoughts • Having the power to convince
Leadership and Charisma:	• Having the ability to motivate a group toward a goal • Using enthusiasm and charm

Observation and Perceptiveness Activities

Observation and perceptiveness begins with the student and their abilities to pay attention to details in interactions, use these details to draw conclusions and find the why, and make correct judgments related to the interaction.

Long Looks

Have students think about/discuss what they know about Sherlock Holmes or another detective. In order to solve a case, they must be able to observe as many details as possible in a short period of time and make connections to what they know. Show the student a piece of artwork (e.g., *A Sunday Afternoon* by Georges Saurat) and have them take a "long look" at it. Give them 45–60 seconds to observe the painting. When time is up, take the painting away and have the student recall as many details as they can. Show the painting again and have the student make inferences about what and why things are happening in this painting. Suggested questions to ask are:

❏ Why would the artist depict the people in this way?
❏ What are some important details that add to the theme of the painting that you might not see at first?
❏ How does this relate to a time when you might not have observed all the details of a situation?
❏ How do the minor details add to the mood of the painting? What could have been left out?

Human Emotion Art Observation

Choose and display a famous portrait (e.g., *Mona Lisa* by da Vinci; *Girl with the Pearl Earring* by Vermeer; *American Gothic* by Wood). Have students use their observation skills to examine the human emotion being portrayed within the painting. Encourage students to be creative in their explanation and use details they find to defend their ideas. For example, one might discuss the farmers in *American Gothic* and share how they just lost their last cow. They might explain how the cow was stolen by a neighboring farm and what they plan to do to get it back.

Situation Replays

Have students explain a recent difficult interaction they have had. This interaction could have been with peers, teachers, or family members and must have been in-person. As students recall the situation, have them explain all of the things they observed about the person they were interacting with (e.g., facial expressions, body language, time of day, previous encounters). Ask them to make inferences about what caused these details to occur. Encourage them to choose a detail to observe the next time they are having a difficult interaction, and challenge them to use the detail to help drive their actions. For example, a student might observe that the teacher they were speaking to was grading papers while they were talking and did not seem fully engaged in their conversation. The student could then find time to discuss their needs when the teacher was not engaged in other tasks.

Leadership Skills Activities

Leadership skills may involve the student speaking and listening to others, but, intrapersonally, the student must be hard-working, responsible, have integrity, and be purpose driven. The following activities are ideas for helping students develop these skills.

My Idea of a Leader

Discuss with students what qualities they think a good leader has. Make a record of these, have students categorize the qualities, and discuss which qualities they think they have and which ones they would like to build. For example, students may identify the qualities of honesty, fairness, and empathy and categorize these as "Treatment of Others."

Great Leader Quick Study

Choose a famous leader students admire. Print a quick biography of the leader and have students complete a Quick Study (i.e., a quick and condensed research project) of the famous leader's leadership skills. Discuss what qualities influenced their ability to become a leader and how they used their leadership skills to impact change. Have students make connections to their own lives and reflect on what leadership skills they possess and how they can better use these skills in their everyday life.

Find My Purpose

Ask students to write or discuss these prompts: What I love; What excites me; What I would change; What makes me feel most like me. Using these prompts, have the students begin narrowing down what their purpose or contribution to the world might be. For example, they may find they want to influence social change. Knowing this purpose can direct them to find opportunities to be a leader.

Motivations and Values

As a person walks the journey of life, what they value most determines the direction they will go. The values humans will not compromise drive their motivation. These are what makes someone think a task is worth doing. After using the "Know Thyself" Core Values Checklist (see Resource 4.4) in Chapter 4, students understand what it is that they value the most. In adolescence, these values may not yet be fully developed, but the student should have an understanding of at least three things they do not want to compromise on.

The Most Valuable Purchase activity (see Resource 5.2) is geared toward encouraging gifted and high-potential students to see how their values relate to their futures and how those values can motivate them to set and pursue valuable goals. This activity can be used one-on-one or with a whole group. For the activity, the teacher provides the student with a copy of Resource 5.2. This shows a list containing positive intangibles of life that the student can "bid" on. The teacher tells the student that they have $2,000 imaginary dollars to bid on any of the items on the list. The teacher then gives the student time to decide which items they will bid on and calculate how much they would be willing to spend on those items. There is no limit to the amount of items they can bid on, as long as their total does not exceed $2,000. After the student has calculated their bids, the teacher and student can begin discussing the items the student chose and how they determined the amount they would spend. The student should then discuss the reflection questions with the teacher. If this intervention is used as a whole group activity, the teacher can hold an actual auction of the items. The items will go to the highest bidder and may only be purchased once. Students may not get what they value the most, so they have to decide on what else they would want to spend their money on.

In this exercise, the teacher leads the student to see how their values drive their motivation for purchasing the items. This is the case in life as well. What a person values the most will determine what they are motivated to do in their life. When a student understands their values and what they are motivated by, they can better map out their journey of life.

RESOURCE 5.2
Most Valuable Purchase

Name: _____

Directions: You have $2,000 to bid on any of the items. You may bid on as many as you would like, and you must spend all of your money. When complete, discuss the questions below.

Be a famous rock star Bid_____	Always be healthy Bid_____	Be extremely smart Bid_____	Be a famous athlete Bid_____
Be very beautiful Bid_____	Be President of the USA Bid_____	Have an attractive body Bid_____	Have 1 million YouTube followers Bid_____
Be a school teacher Bid_____	Graduate from a prestigious college Bid_____	Always have clear skin Bid_____	Help underprivileged children Bid_____
Have a successful medical career Bid_____	Be a successful politician Bid_____	Raise a happy family Bid_____	Be a celebrated artist Bid_____

Reflection
1. Why were you willing to bid more on some items than others?
2. What do your highest bids tell you about what you value most in life?
3. Do you think others would have bid on your top items? Why or why not?
4. Is there something <u>not</u> on the list you would be willing to spend all your money on?
5. How can you relate your bids to your school career?
6. Do your top items make you want to work harder? Discuss your answer.

Personality Traits

A gifted or high-potential student's personality traits can have a great impact on their ability to find and utilize their talents. When students have a closed mind or are closed off to new experiences, they are unable to broaden their thinking and encounter novel situations where they can learn and grow. Students who are not conscientious with their schoolwork, extracurricular activities, and other responsibilities in or out of school will find that they are passed over for or miss opportunities that could have made a significant impact in their life. Social skills and a level of student agency are both required for a student to achieve their goals. Students must be able to show respect and trust others, be trustworthy themselves, and have compassion for those around them. They must also have self-regulation skills and the ability to stabilize emotions, especially in times of extreme anxiety. While a student's personality will not fully change, below are some suggested activities (see Table 5.3) geared toward strengthening intrapersonal awareness and improving traits that cause distinct barriers in life.

Links Between Neuroticism, Perfectionism, and Resilience

In studies about perfectionism and personality, a link has been made to neuroticism (Flett et al., 1989). When gifted students focus more on their failures than their successes, they exhibit unhealthy perfectionism (Mofield & Parker Peters, 2018b). They have a preoccupation with increasingly high standards, which can lead to negative self-perception and increased anxiety. In order to combat this unhealthy perfectionism and neuroticism, the student should learn strategies for determining what is realistic and what they can control. An assessment of the student's internal locus of control can be done, but the teacher can also use My Focus of Control (see Resource 5.3) to help the student explore what is in their control and what is not.

Using Resource 5.3, the teacher and student discuss a particular situation that is currently happening with the student, a situation that has happened in the past, or as an overall view of the student's life. In this exercise, the teacher should have the student recount the situation aloud. As the student tells of the problems that have come from the situation or the feelings that arose, they should record these in the category in which they fall: things I can control or things I cannot control. The teacher guides

TABLE 5.3
Strengthening Intrapersonal Skills Through Personality

Openness	Conscientiousness	Extroversion	Agreeableness	Neuroticism
Question your own bias. Find sources that contradict your opinions.	Recognize the purpose you are working toward.	Have regular conversations with peers and teachers.	Seek out a role model who exhibits this personality type.	Be proactive instead of reactive. Think "I can do this."
Recognize what you don't know. There is a big world to discover.	Be mindful in what you are working on. Explore a mindfulness practice.	Recognize that what you have to say is important.	Take an interest in the people you interact with each day.	Have a thought-out plan for when things go wrong.
Be curious and ask questions. Learn from others' perspectives.	Break down tasks into smaller chunks. Make a to-do list.	Set small goals to get outside your comfort zone.	Make a shortlist of things you are grateful for each day.	Avoid "catastrophizing" the situation. Consider what is real.
Say "yes" to new experiences and interactions.	Celebrate each success—no matter how tiny. This will build your confidence.	Listen to the other person; wait until they are finished to speak.	Evaluate what you plan to say to avoid insults and hurtful comments.	Use Box Breathing or other mindfulness methods when in distress.

the student to realize that most things are not within their control. What they can control is how they proceed with what has happened. Knowing that most things are not within their control can help them see if they are proactive in the situation or reacting to the situation. They should also find that these things happen to everyone. Perfectionists and neurotic personalities worry about the future and what they cannot control. Proactive people are curious about why bad things happen, ask questions to learn more, anticipate other problems that may arise, and make a plan for what to do in the face of adversity. Students learn to be proactive in their lives by working through this process and are empowered to become more resilient. See Table 5.4 for additional strategies to use with students who exhibit high anxiety.

TABLE 5.4

Additional Strategies for High Anxiety

Anxiety Situation	Strategy to Employ
Anxiety when performing in front of others (e.g., speaking up in class, sports, competitions)	Ask the question, "Who cares?" This is not asked in a flippant way, but in a curious way. Do the people present really care if I make a small mistake? Will their view of me really change? The answer is usually that a mistake will not make any difference in how you are perceived, especially if you use that mistake to make yourself better. When feeling anxious about performing, ask "Who cares?"
General anxiety relating to perfectionism	Move your body for a period of time each day. Physical exercise has shown great effects on anxiety in adolescents (Klizine et al., 2018). Go for a walk, run, or bike ride. Write out a 5–10-minute workout plan or follow an exercise video online. A small amount of movement each day will compound over time and reduce general anxiety.
Anxiety in a social situation	Prepare yourself for a social situation with positive self-talk. Give yourself one to two phrases that you can repeat about yourself to increase your self-confidence and redirect your focus in the situation. For example, "My opinions matter. I am as important as everyone else." These mantras should be repeated any time anxious feelings surface.

RESOURCE 5.3
My Focus of Control

Name: _____

Directions: Within the smaller shaded circle, write down things that are absolutely in your control at school, home, and in other activities. Within the larger circle, write down things that are not in your control at school, home, and in other activities. Think about how this realization can impact how you react in these areas.

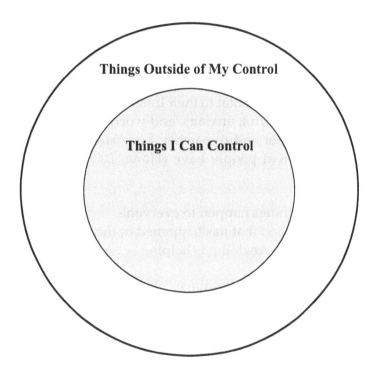

Reflection

1. What are some things you try to control that are not in your hands?
2. Which thing were you relieved to find was not something you can control?
3. When you worry about something that is not yours to control, what can you do to remember to be proactive instead of reactive?

Developing Resilience

When talking with gifted and high-potential students, a common theme that often comes up in discussion is all of the terrible things that are happening to them. This negative thinking is a type of catastrophizing, imagining and ruminating on the worst-possible outcome. Gifted and high-potential students can easily become fixated on receiving a bad grade, on others making fun of them if they give a wrong answer, or on not being accepted into the college they have always dreamed of. Tuning in to their feelings and thoughts helps the student understand that the catastrophe is not what will happen in real life and that they will recover if something bad happens. This self-awareness increases the student's resiliency.

A student is said to be resilient when they can bounce back from adversity. However, gifted students often do not have to actually encounter that adversity for it to be detrimental to their lives. Just imagining the outcome can cause them to be fearful, anxious, and worried, as in catastrophizing above. Resiliency author and researcher, Lucy Hone, explains that there are three traits resilient people have (Hone, 2020). She suggests that resilient people:

1. Realize that bad things happen to everyone.
2. Think about the good that has happened in the situation.
3. Decide if what they are doing is helping or harming themselves.

The Resiliency Strategy (see Resource 5.4) is based on these three skills. In this resource, the teacher and student work through these traits and use them as an ongoing strategy to support the student in becoming more resilient.

RESOURCE 5.4
Resiliency Strategy

Name: _____

What bad thing has happened to me? Who else has had something like this happen to them?	What are the good things I can see in this situation? What things can I control?	How am I reacting to this situation? Is this helping me? How can I be proactive?

Note: Adapted from Hone (2020).

Reflection
1. Rebounding after a tough situation can build your resiliency. Discuss a time similar to this situation where you were able to manage the situation and be ok.
2. Pretend your friend is in this situation instead of you. What advice would you give your friend?
3. Can you use the advice you would give a friend? If not, how can you tweak it to work for you?

Increasing Student Volition

The popular saying, "How do you eat an elephant? One bite at a time," comes to mind when thinking about the planning and follow-through that comes with schoolwork. Projects, homework, and even large tasks that a student enjoys can become very overwhelming. Frequently, students complain that they do not know where to begin or feel that they are never going to complete all of the work. This often leads to extreme procrastination. Extreme procrastination may cause the student to fall behind and fear failure in the task. The fear of failure can cause the student to think that they would rather get a zero for the assignment than have what effort they do give receive a poor grade. This cycle can lead to underachievement for a gifted student, and, worse, they never learn to plan and follow through with meaningful tasks. Without this skill, our gifted and high-potential students are not able to show what they know and fulfill the potential they have. Students must be taught how to eat the elephant one bite at a time.

Gifted and high-potential students who have barriers in volition may need to learn to plan their tasks, how to prepare themselves and their environments in order to complete the task, and self-regulate in order to follow through with their plans. They may also have difficulty increasing their motivation to finish tasks during the process. Using the Task Planning Guide (Resource 5.5), teachers guide students in planning for the tasks they take on and support them in gaining the skills necessary to complete tasks regularly. In the Task Planning Guide, the student identifies the task at hand, sets the due date, plans out the steps required and schedules these, identifies ways to motivate themself, plans for setting up their environment to reduce distractions, and then reflects on why they are completing the task. This can be part of the PEGS process as the teacher and student use these sections to create short-term goals for the student within this larger plan. Increasing the student's volition will contribute to many other facets of their life. They will be more likely to recognize ways they can make themself successful when they are regularly using this resource as a guide. As the student internalizes these strategies, they will be empowered to problem-solve and plan out tasks in the future.

RESOURCE 5.5
Task Planning Guide

Name: _____

Identify the Task:	Task Steps and Dates
Task Due Date:	
Motivation Tools I Can Use • • •	
Plan for My Environment • • • • •	
What's In It For Me?	

Task Valuation

Gifted and high-potential students learn a lot about themselves when they evaluate what motivates them in different situations. The Task Valuation Decision Tree (Resource 5.6) was developed using Expectancy-Value Theory (Wigfield & Eccles, 2000). Using the Task Valuation Decision Tree as a guide, the student and teacher begin to discuss what motivates the student to complete tasks, set goals, follow through with commitments, and even identify why they procrastinate on certain tasks. This also leads to the student better understanding where their strengths lie and what goals should be set that will positively impact their future.

Teachers can also use the Task Valuation Hexagonal Thinking Activity (see Resource 5.7) with students in order to gain more knowledge of their values, wants, and barriers. In this activity, the teacher cuts apart the hexagons and gives students the opportunity to write things they value (e.g., excellence), things they want to do in their lives (e.g., attend college), things they are interested in (e.g., marine biology), and barriers they are currently facing (e.g., lacking self-advocacy). The students must complete at least 12–15 hexagons. Students think through connections that can be made between the hexagons and place sides together to illustrate the link. For example, a student's interest in marine biology might be connected to their desire to attend a college that specializes in that field. In turn, this also connects to the student's value of excellence, which encourages the student to self-advocate for additional opportunities in this area. In this example, the student's value, desire, and barrier would all connect to their interest in marine biology. The hexagons would visually appear in more of a flower shape than a straight line as students connect multiple sides of each hexagon. Students verbalize and justify all links between the hexagons to either the teacher or their partner. This activity encourages gifted and high-potential students to recognize where their values lie and their purpose for goal setting.

RESOURCE 5.6
Task Valuation Decision Tree

Name: _____

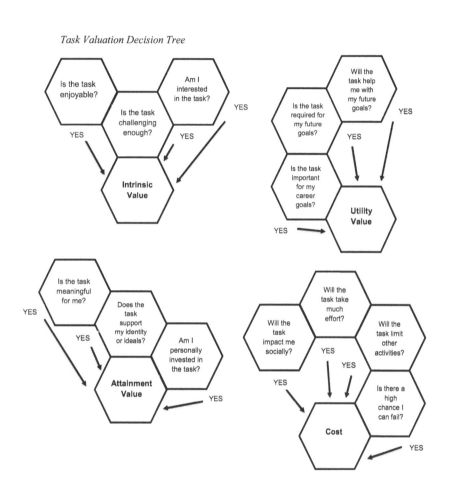

Task Valuation Decision Tree

Reflection
1. After reviewing the decision tree, choose a task to evaluate. Examples: homework, sport or band practice, chores at home.
2. Discuss which types of tasks fall into each valuation category for you.
3. Which type of valuation are you using when you feel most motivated? Least?

RESOURCE 5.7
Task Valuation Hexagonal Thinking Activity

Name: _____

Directions

1. Cut out each hexagon. On individual hexagons, write things that you value, things you want to do in your life, things you are interested in, and barriers you are facing now.
2. Think about how these pieces of your life connect. Connect the hexagons on as many sides as possible. Justify your connections with your teacher or partner.

Psychosocial Skills

During the adolescent years, it is expected that students should be able to direct their activity to accomplishing tasks, learn how to navigate and function within a social group, and be able to contribute well to the group (Chung, 2018). They should also be moving toward having regulated bodies and minds and be able to be independent. Gifted and high-potential learners may have high aptitudes in some of these areas. However, for some, asynchronous development may cause them to develop these psychosocial skills more slowly than their peers (Rakow, 2020). Table 5.5, Strategies for

TABLE 5.5

Strategies for Building Psychosocial Skills

Skill Area	Strategies to Try
Self-confidence within a group	• Employ positive self-talk: Choose two to three phrases to regularly say to yourself. Write these phrases down and place them when you can see them throughout the day. • Start a mindfulness practice. Find time to meditate or use breathing exercises to promote confidence and reduce anxiety. • Write in a journal after work within a group or other type of social situation. Write three things that you did well during that session and one thing you plan to work on next time. • Before entering a group setting, rehearse a few things that you plan to say and picture how you will say them.
Emotional regulation (also adapting to change)	• Use Box Breathing (i.e., breathe in for four seconds, hold for four seconds, breathe out for four seconds, hold for four seconds, repeat three to four cycles) or the 4-7-8 Breathing Method (i.e., breathe in for four seconds, hold for seven seconds, breathe out slowly for eight seconds, repeat four cycles) to calm overwhelming feelings and refocus on the tasks at hand. • Acknowledge the feelings and let them float away like a cloud. This type of mindfulness validates the feelings but keeps them from becoming too overwhelming. • Imagine scenarios that could happen and follow them to their outcome. For example, if you are becoming anxious about a test, imagine that you do poorly on the test. Think through what could happen because of this and how important this would be in the entirety of your life. While there are consequences you may have to overcome, you will be ok.

(continued)

TABLE 5.5 (Continued)
Strategies for Building Psychosocial Skills

Skill Area	Strategies to Try
Organization of materials	• Have a "home" for everything you will use or receive throughout the day. Specific folders for homework, places for your pens, a location for your backpack at home, dividers for classroom materials. • Use the OHIO Method: Only Handle It Once. When in contact with a piece of material that needs to be put away, put it in its correct spot the first time so you only have to worry about it one time. • Start a morning and afternoon routine for your materials. For example, in the morning, I check that my homework, lunchbox, and water bottle are in my backpack before leaving home. In the afternoon, I check that these same things are in my backpack before I leave school.
Time management	• Make a list of your tasks. Whether you like to have a calendar or just a running "to-do" list, record the incoming tasks as soon as possible. Paper/notebook planners can be useful, as well as to-do list applications for devices. • Regularly schedule an amount of time to complete tasks. Tack this time onto another habit in order to promote follow through. For example, when I get home in the afternoons, I will get a snack and begin my homework. • Put easily completed tasks on your to-do list and do these tasks first. Marking off small tasks will build momentum and motivate you to complete larger tasks.
Study skills	• Learn how to take notes. There are many tutorials online or you can ask a teacher or parent. Types of note-taking include: Cornell Notes, Outlines, Sketch-noting, and Mind Maps. • Use your notes to power flashcards or other study materials you make. Combine important concepts or ideas from the text with your notes to create a full understanding of the material. • Use self-testing strategies in order to prepare for exams. Using notes, flashcards, online resources, and textbooks, find a self-testing method that works for you. • Schedule a time to study. Studying in the classroom before the teacher hands out the exam is usually inadequate. Schedule time for a few nights before the exam to study for short intervals. This will increase the likelihood of retaining the information.

Building Psychosocial Skills, provides ideas for encouraging development of psychosocial skills in the classroom setting. During the PEGS process, when students recognize improvements need to be made in these areas, the teacher guides them to set goals and employ these strategies.

Inner Dialogue and Mindset

The mind is a powerful tool that can motivate a person to succeed or overwhelm the person into failure. What a student says to themself is an important part of self-regulation and achievement of goals (Bülbül & Akyol, 2020). Self-talk can either be positive or negative, either encouraging a behavior or judging a behavior using discouraging expressions. These types of inner dialogue can play an immense role in a student's performance at school, in sports, and in extracurricular activities. How they speak to themself can influence how they speak to others and how they think others perceive them. It is important for gifted and high-potential learners to discover the power of their minds, how they currently speak to themselves in different types of situations, and how to have control over their thoughts.

The Power of the Mind

In the Power of the Mind activity (see Resource 5.8), students experience how their thoughts impact their actions. First, the teacher provides the student with a flat metal washer, ring, or object attached to a string. The student holds this in front of their own face without their arm touching anything. It will look like the student is trying to hypnotize themself. The teacher instructs the student to hold the washer completely still and try to make it move using only their eyes. The student repeats the phrase "left to right" over and over as they hold the washer. They will see the washer begin to move in that direction. They can try this again using the phrase "back and forth" and repeating it. After the student has done this activity, the teacher and student discuss the reflection questions. The student realizes that their mind has power. They begin examining how they speak to themself in different types of situations. The teacher facilitates realization of what things can be positive and what can influence them negatively.

RESOURCE 5.8

The Power of the Mind

Name: _____

Directions: Using a metal washer on a string, follow the steps to experiment with your mind powers.

Step 1	Hold the washer in front of your face so that you can focus your eyes on it. Make sure your arm is not touching anything. At first, only focus on keeping the washer still.
Step 2	Hold the washer still. Using only your eyes, focus your mind to make the washer move.
Step 3	Repeat aloud or in your head the words "left to right" over and over and see what happens.
Step 4	Repeat aloud or in your head the words "back to front" over and over and see what happens.

Reflection

1. What happened to the washer when you didn't say anything?
2. What happened to the washer when you repeated the directions? Why do you think this happened?
3. When is a time that you talk to yourself or repeat things to yourself?
4. When you talk to yourself, would you say that you encourage yourself or say things that are discouraging?
5. How do these types of self-talk impact you? Describe a time when what you said to yourself was helpful and/or harmful.

Developing a Growth Mindset

Whether the gifted or high-potential student falls into the category of fixed mindset or growth mindset, it is important that curricula are appropriately challenging for them. These students require challenges that produce a productive struggle as they learn (Mofield & Parker Peters, 2018a). These learning struggles build their endurance for growing in other challenging situations. If students lean more toward having a fixed mindset in one or more areas, they should be instructed on how the brain learns and how they can apply this to the areas of struggle. Growing the Mind (see Resource 5.9) is a research activity for the student to explore how the brain learns new material and to make connections to their lives.

RESOURCE 5.9
Growing the Mind

Name: _____

Directions: Search for how you can grow your intelligence and read research about the brain. Complete the organizer with the information you find. Then complete the questions below.

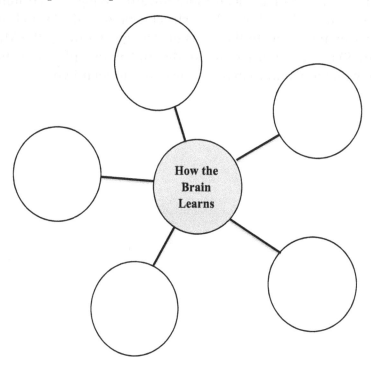

How the Brain Learns

How is the brain like a muscle?	Why are neuron connections important?	When have you practiced something and succeeded?

Continuing Through the PEGS Model

As the teacher and student move through the Purposeful Empowerment in Goal Setting process, the important first step is to understand and address any intrapersonal strengths and struggles the student is facing. The goal-setting team can then collect and evaluate strategies to strengthen the areas needed to succeed. The intrapersonal information and strategies will then support the interpersonal skills and application of these skills to the student's learning as the team proceeds with the model. Student reflection in each of these areas will be addressed more in Chapter 8. However, it is important to note that self-reflection is constantly occurring in this process. Student self-reflection will trigger thoughts and ideas they have about themself and will set boundaries for what strategies they generate for improvement. The PEGS Model requires constant reflection and self-awareness in order to empower the students.

References

Bülbül, A., & Akyol, G. (2020). The effect of self-talk on athletes. *African Educational Research Journal, 8*(3), 640–648. https://doi.org/10.30918/AERJ.83.20.141

Bandura, A. (1986). *Social foundations of thought and action: A social cognitive theory*. Prentice Hall.

Chung, D. Y. (2018). The eight stages of psychosocial protective development: Developmental psychology. *Journal of Behavioral and Brain Science, 8*, 369–398. https://doi.org/10.4236/jbbs.2018.86024

Flett, G. L., Hewitt, P. L., & Dyck, D. G. (1989). Self-oriented perfectionism, neuroticism and anxiety. *Personality and Individual Differences, 10*(7), 731–735. https://doi.org/10.1016/0191-8869(89)90119-0

Gagné, F. (2021). *Differentiating giftedness from talent: The DMGT perspective on talent development*. Routledge.

Hone, L. (2020). *3 secrets of resilient people*. TED. www.ted.com/speakers/lucy_hone.

Kliziene, I., Sipaviciene, S., Cizauskas, G., & Klizas, S. (2018). Effects of a 7-month exercise intervention programme on the psychosocial adjustment and decrease of anxiety among adolescents. *European Journal of Contemporary Education, 7*(1), 127–136. https://doi.org/10.13187/ejced.2018.1.127

Mofield, E. L., & Parker Peters, M. (2018a). Mindset misconception? Comparing mindsets, perfectionism, and attitudes of achievement in gifted, advanced, and typical students. *Gifted Child Quarterly, 62*(4), 327–349. https://doi.org/10.1177/0016986218758440

Mofield, E. L., & Parker Peters, M. (2018b). Shifting the perfectionistic mindset: Moving to mindful excellence. *Gifted Child Today, 41*(4), 177–185.

Parsi, A., Whittaker, M. C., & Jones, L. E. (2018). *Agents of their own success: Self-advocacy skills and self-determination for students with disabilities in the era of personalized learning.* National Center for Learning Disabilities. www.ncld.org/wp-content/uploads/2018/03/Agents-of-Their-Own-Success_Final.pdf

Rakow, S. (2020). *Educating gifted students in middle school.* Routledge.

Sørlie, M.-A., Hagen, K. A., & Nordahl, K. B. (2020). Development of social skills during middle childhood: Growth trajectories and school-related predictors. *International Journal of School & Educational Psychology, 9*(sup1), S69–S87. https://doi.org/10.1080/21683603.2020.1744492

Wigfield, A., & Eccles, J. S. (2000). Expectancy-value theory of achievement motivation. *Contemporary Educational Psychology, 25*(1), 68–81. https://doi.org/10.1006/ceps.1999.1015

Zedan, R., & Bitar, J. (2017). Mathematically gifted students: Their characteristics and unique needs. *European Journal of Education Studies, 3*(4). https://doi.org/10.5281/zenodo.37595

CHAPTER 6

Express Thyself

The Second Stage of Goal Development

Interpersonal skills are paramount in the goal-development process, as they serve as the bridge from intrapersonal awareness to effectively communicating one's needs. As discussed in Chapter 5, gifted and high-potential learners first need to understand their personal strengths, values, and needs to effectively set purposeful goals. After students begin to recognize and apply this heightened level of self-awareness to identifying a goal, the next step is to begin to develop a plan for how to communicate their needs toward achieving that goal.

All too often, people hear the word "communication" and only think of the verbal aptitude required to effectively convey an idea, need, or question. Purposeful Empowerment in Goal Setting (PEGS) recognizes that communication encompasses a great deal more than that. In essence, interpersonal skills include communication skills that extend beyond verbal behaviors, including nonverbal behaviors, committed listening, problem-solving, conflict resolution, and adapting to new situations. All of these interpersonal skills act as the conduit for interacting with various stakeholders throughout the goal-attainment process. By working through the PEGS Model, gifted and high-potential students not only learn how to apply their interpersonal skills to successfully achieve their goals, they also develop essential skills needed to effectively navigate our diverse, global world.

DOI: 10.4324/9781003331049-7

Key Components of Communication

Gagné (2021) signifies interpersonal dynamics through the environment component within the Differentiating Model of Giftedness and Talent (DMGT). As such, key stakeholders involved in the talent development process are identified as parents, teachers/mentors, and peers. When exploring the role of interpersonal dynamics on the goal-development process, these stakeholders are key figures that impact how a goal is developed and actualized and naturally become considerations of who students need to effectively communicate with to achieve their goals.

More specifically, through identifying key stakeholders, gifted and high-potential students begin to learn how to engage in respectful communication and recognize the multiple perspectives involved in the communication process. To continue supporting them through the PEGS process, we have categorized interpersonal skills into the following key components of communication:

- ❏ Verbal/Nonverbal Communication Skills
- ❏ Committed Listening
- ❏ Problem-Solving
- ❏ Conflict Resolution
- ❏ Adapting to New Situations

The PEGS Model classifies these into Foundational Communication Skills and Application-Based Communication Skills (see Table 6.1), providing a greater understanding of how each contributes to the goal-development and attainment process.

The Foundations of Effective Communication

At the core of effective communication are the foundations of verbal/nonverbal communication and committed listening skills. These interpersonal skills are integral to not only communicating one's needs, but also to applying these skills within a real-world context. Without a doubt, these foundational communication skills are also at the center of collaborating with others, being a strong leader, and navigating our global world.

While the following sections will provide a generalized overview of these interpersonal skills as they relate to effective communication and goal attainment, we have also included a variety of activities that can be used to further develop these skills in a variety of instructional approaches

TABLE 6.1
Foundational and Application-Based Communication Skills

Classification of Communication Skills	Type of Communication Skill	Key Connections to Goal Development and Attainment
Foundational Communication Skills: *These interpersonal skills are the foundation of core communication and are essential components to the application of communicating with others*	Verbal/Nonverbal Communication	• Effectively communicate needs, ideas, and/or questions • Remain mindful of body language (e.g., gestures, posture, eye contact) when communicating messages • Recognize how tone of voice, manner of speaking, and mindset related to communication impact how others receive intended messages
	Committed Listening	• Recognize how committed listening plays an integral role in knowing how to proceed with effective communication • Increase awareness of how inner dialogue may impact the degree to which communication is heard and understood • Understand that committed listening is a key interpersonal skill that continues to inform next steps in communication
Application-Based Communication Skills: *These interpersonal skills encompass foundational communication skills as applied in a variety of real-world applications of practice*	Problem-Solving	• Leverage foundational communication skills to find new solutions • Recognize the role of flexibility in communication and mindset to address complex situations in the goal attainment process
	Conflict Resolution	• Understand how to resolve disagreements through foundational communication skills • Recognize multiple perspectives to better navigate effective communication • Remain cognizant of how a threat to core values impedes effective communication • Understand the importance of respectful discourse resolving conflict
	Adapting to New Situations	• Recognize how effective communication supports adapting to new situations • Incorporate foundational communication skills as a means to understand unexpected events and potential barriers to achieving established goals

TABLE 6.2
Activities to Strengthen Interpersonal Communication Skills

Interpersonal Skill Development Area (Special Note: All activities include multiple interpersonal skills but are listed by focused skill development area.)	Activity
Verbal/Nonverbal Communication Skills	• 20 Questions through PPI • A Picture is Worth a Thousand Words • Accountable Talk Scenarios • Actions Speak Louder Than Words
Active Listening	• I'm All Ears! • The "Right" of Passage
Problem-Solving	• Does It All Add Up? • It's Time for a Sit-In • Linking It All Together
Conflict Resolution	• All Torn Up • Conflict Resolution Spiral
Adapting to New Situations	• A Recipe for Successful Change • Moving in New Directions

(e.g., one-on-one, partner work, small/whole group). When reading through these sections, it is important to recognize that communication skills do not happen in isolation. Most of these activities incorporate a variety of skills, but are categorized in this chapter according to the primary communication skill being developed (see Table 6.2). The latter part of this chapter will provide an overview of how these interpersonal skills are directly aligned with goal setting through the second stage of the PEGS Model.

Verbal/Nonverbal Communication Skills

Goals are often impacted and attained through effective communication with others. As such, gifted and high-potential learners need opportunities to further develop their verbal and nonverbal communication skills. In terms of leadership, natural born leaders are often associated with having the verbal ease to communicate their needs and visions with others. Gagné (2021) describes these verbal skills as being on a vertical axis. Likewise, he recognizes that there are nonverbal interpersonal factors that equally

TABLE 6.3

Interpersonal Communication Quadrants

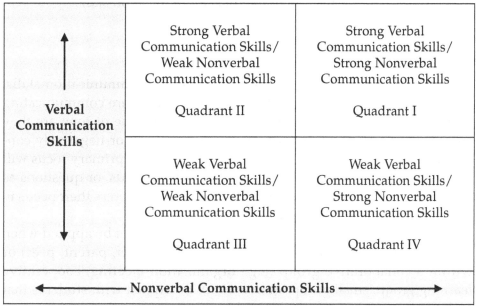

	Strong Verbal Communication Skills/ Weak Nonverbal Communication Skills Quadrant II	Strong Verbal Communication Skills/ Strong Nonverbal Communication Skills Quadrant I
Verbal Communication Skills		
	Weak Verbal Communication Skills/ Weak Nonverbal Communication Skills Quadrant III	Weak Verbal Communication Skills/ Strong Nonverbal Communication Skills Quadrant IV
	◄──────── **Nonverbal Communication Skills** ────────►	

impact effective communication, and he places these on a horizontal axis (see Table 6.3).

In referencing Table 6.3, the ultimate goal is for students to develop interpersonal skills that fall within Quadrant I. Students who fall into this quadrant typically have a strong self-awareness and ability to relate to others. These students are typically strong leaders who understand the importance of knowing when to speak, when to listen, and how to navigate the complexities of nonverbal social cues. To the other extreme, students who fall within Quadrant III need significant support in developing both verbal and nonverbal interpersonal skills, and students in the remaining quadrants demonstrate strengths in either verbal or nonverbal communication skills, but not both. For *every* student, it is important to leverage their strengths as they address areas of need.

In terms of how these skills impact the goal-development process, it is somewhat dependent on the goal that is being developed. For example, if a student's goal is to develop stronger self-advocacy skills, then both verbal and nonverbal communication skills will greatly impact the degree to which that student will be able to achieve their goal. If, instead, the student's goal is focused on independent study skills, then the verbal and nonverbal communication skills will still be a factor, but not be as integral. While gifted and high-potential learners continue to develop their intrapersonal awareness (see Chapter 5) in regard to their interpersonal skills, the following sections provide suggestions for activities to further develop students' verbal and nonverbal communication skills.

Activities to Strengthen Verbal/Nonverbal Communication Skills

When working to develop verbal and nonverbal communication skills, students will, in large part, be focusing on *how* they are communicating with others. What are their chosen words? What type of tone are they speaking in? How is their body language positively or negatively contributing to the message they are trying to send? The primary focus will be on *how* to effectively communicate their ideas, needs, or questions as related to their goals. In essence, how will students express their needs to successfully achieve their goals?

It is important to understand that these skills might be applied when communicating with just one individual (e.g., teacher, parent, peer) or within a collaborative group (e.g., organization meeting, cooperative learning group, small group intervention). Be explicit with students that verbal/nonverbal communications do not happen in isolation; they work in tandem. The following are suggested activities to strengthen the verbal/ nonverbal interpersonal skills needed to successfully navigate the goal-attainment process.

20 Questions Through Presuming Positive Intent (PPI)

Respectful discourse is at the root of communication through Presuming Positive Intent (PPI). When we lead our communications through presuming positive intent, we communicate in a respectful manner that lets those we are communicating with feel capable, knowledgeable, and well-intentioned (Kee et al., 2010). Through this strength-based approach to seeking out positive interactions, questions are phrased in an open-ended manner vs. a yes/no response. Not only does this maintain a solutions-focused conversation, it also steers away from making someone feel inferior or disrespected. For example, if a well-intentioned gifted student is trying to self-advocate for more challenging work and asks the teacher, "Because I've been doing really well with this unit, have you thought about providing more challenging work for me to complete?" the teacher might feel as though the student is implying that they are not doing their job. After all, it *is* the teacher's job to differentiate for their students. Instead, if the gifted student communicates through PPI, the question

TABLE 6.4

Presuming Positive Intent Sentence Stems

Instead of...	Consider...
• Can you...? • Could you...? • Did you...? • Do you...? • Have you...?	• As someone who...? • Given...? • In what ways...? • What...? • When...? • Which...?
Because I've been doing really well with this unit, **have you** *thought about providing more challenging work for me to complete?*	*Because I've been doing really well with this unit,* **what** *topics within this unit might provide me with new opportunities to go deeper in my learning?*

Note: Adapted from Kee et al. (2010)

might resemble, "Because I've been doing really well with this unit, what topics within this unit might provide me with new opportunities to go deeper in my learning?" Through this question, the gifted student is respecting the teacher's content knowledge and ability to support them through more challenging learning opportunities. It provides the context for making proactive plans for next steps.

Through the 20 Questions for PPI activity, gifted and high-potential learners are tasked with brainstorming 20 questions through the lens of PPI that are focused on helping them achieve their goals. For example, in the above example of self-advocacy, gifted and high-potential students will see if they can create 20 different questions that might be utilized across a variety of settings/situations, related to that self-advocacy goal. These questions might be geared toward interactions with teachers, the students' own personal reflections, or even peers and parents. Communicating through PPI takes practice, and this is a great way for gifted and high-potential learners to think broadly about their goals and how to communicate with others through proactive, solutions-focused communications. Table 6.4 provides a list of PPI sentence stems to support gifted and high-potential students in this task.

A Picture Is Worth a Thousand Words

With a strong focus on communicating effectively and purposefully, this activity provides gifted and high-potential students with an opportunity

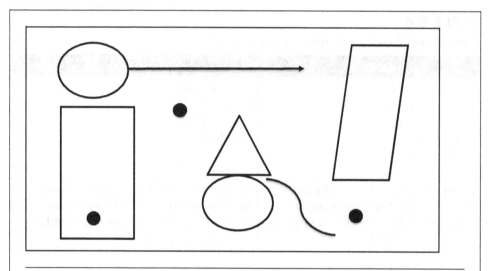

Figure 6.1 Sample Geometric Drawing for *A Picture is Worth a Thousand Words* Activity

to learn how to formulate their thoughts and communicate a directed message without being able to read any additional body language. For this activity, students will be paired and asked to sit back to back with their partner. (If this activity is being done one-on-one with a teacher and student, they will also sit back to back.) One student is given a blank piece of paper, a pencil, and a hard surface (e.g., clipboard) to write on, and the other student is given a geometric drawing (see Figure 6.1). The student with the drawn picture has to communicate to their partner what to draw *without* letting them see the picture and *without* seeing what their partner is drawing. The student drawing the picture is not allowed to ask any questions. They must solely rely on the verbal description from their partner. Once the drawing is "complete," students should reflect (see Table 6.5) on the experience before switching roles to work through the process again with a different picture.

Accountable Talk Scenarios

Regardless of the setting, respect should be at the foundation of all social interactions. By providing gifted and high-potential learners with the opportunity to practice how to communicate through a respectful lens, verbal/nonverbal skills are greatly strengthened. For this activity, the teacher will need to first identify the parameters surrounding the context

TABLE 6.5

Reflection Prompts for *A Picture is Worth a Thousand Words*

Reflection Prompts for A *Picture is Worth a Thousand Words*
• In comparing the drawings, what aspects of verbal communication contributed to the outcome, either positively or negatively?
• What feelings were associated with each role? Why do you think you felt that way?
• How might this relate to communicating your needs in relation to goals you set for yourself?
• What steps might you be able to implement if you need greater clarity in your own communication or the communication you are receiving from others?

for the "mock" conversations. These conversations might take the form of one-on-one conversations or small group/full-class discussions. In planning for these discussions, the following questions provide key considerations for the teacher as they determine the context or subject matter for the accountable talk scenarios:

❑ What are the key values/concepts that are foundational to the goals being developed (e.g., fairness, time on task, organization of materials, collaboration, specific content mastery)?

❑ How do students' past, present, or future goals relate to the real world?

❑ How might past experiences impact future goal attainment?

❑ Will the student(s) participating in this accountable talk scenario need any additional supports beyond the provided sentence stems (e.g., visuals, flexible seating, manipulatives)?

❑ How will students be supported to stay on task during the accountable talk scenario?

❑ What are possible student responses and how might the teacher address any unexpected responses?

By using these guiding questions, the teacher is able to craft a "big idea" scenario that will help gifted and high-potential students engage in an accountable talk scenario. For example, the teacher might think of a past classroom experience when students had to work collaboratively and ask the students to engage in a reflective conversation with each other through accountable talk. They might discuss what they learned from the activity or how they might approach it differently if given the opportunity, but throughout the group conversation, students will be mindful of respectful discourse. Another option might be to have students focus

TABLE 6.6

Examples of Accountable Talk Sentence Stems

• I agree with _____ because _____.	• I disagree with that because _____.
• I want to add to what (name) said about _____.	• Based on the evidence I have gathered, I think _____.
• I don't know what you mean by _____.	• A question I have is _____.
• This reminds me of _____.	• This is different because _____.
• When we _____, it helped me understand _____.	• What if you had started with _____ rather than _____?
• I'm confused by _____.	• Clarify what you mean by _____.

on a debatable topic currently under study (e.g., which character in a text made the greatest impact) or a global problem (e.g., sustainable resources, global warming). Regardless of the topic, the teacher will share account-able talk sentence stems with the participating students (e.g., projected on wall, handout, separate slips of paper) and students must incorporate those sentence stems into the conversation (see Table 6.6).

Throughout the activity, students focus on respectfully communicating their thoughts through verbal and nonverbal interactions and recognizing how posture, tone of voice, eye contact, and other attentive behaviors impact the goal of the communication. For an additional focus on non-verbal behaviors, provide one student at a time with a nonverbal cue card (e.g., bored, frustrated, excited, highly attentive, argumentative) that they must embody as part of their body language and tone of voice. Students will then reflect on how nonverbal behaviors impact the message even though an accountable talk sentence stem was the actual base of verbal communication. At the conclusion of this activity all students reflect on how verbal/nonverbal communications affect how their message was communicated, received, and contributed to moving the goal of the con-versation forward.

Actions Speak Louder Than Words

In this familiar group activity, students are given 60 seconds to line up according to the order of their birthdays, with the student's birthday closest to January 1 at the beginning of the line and the student whose birthday is closest to December 31 at the end. The only catch is that

TABLE 6.7

Reflection Prompts for *Actions Speak Louder Than Words*

Reflection Prompts for *Actions Speak Louder Than Words*
• What barriers made this activity difficult to complete?
• What actions were most beneficial in communication? Are any of these actions frequently used to clarify verbal communication?
• What "feelings" were evident through the nonverbal communications being used?
• What does this activity teach us about communication, and in particular, how might nonverbal communication impact achieving one's goals?

they can *only* use nonverbal communication. Absolutely no speaking or mouthing of words is permitted. If students are unable to accomplish this task in 60 seconds, allow them an additional attempt before leading them through the reflection questions found in Table 6.7.

Committed Listening

In the field of education, the term "active listening" is often used to signify the importance of being present in the listening process as a means to effectively hear and respond appropriately to the information being shared. With the first stage of PEGS focusing so intently on the importance of intrapersonal awareness (see Chapter 5), *committed* listening is more accurate for the level of listening that the PEGS Model is founded on. This is because the purpose behind active and committed listening is slightly different. For example, active listening, at its core, is needed for effective discussions which require an individual to be listening with an intent to respond through a personal point of view or position (Bohm, 1996), whereas committed listening incorporates the need to listen for understanding vs. strictly listening to respond with evidence (Mofield & Phelps, in press).

Committed listening in regard to goal attainment includes listening for understanding the purpose or intent behind the shared message. Once students are able to recognize the underlying message being communicated, they are better able to recognize how their own personal values connect with the values of the speaker. Through this process of understanding the core message behind a speaker's words, gifted and high-potential learners are more apt to respond through respectful and purposeful dialogue instead of responding with only an understanding of their own perspective. While this is important within many aspects of effective communication, it is especially important when working to resolve conflict with others. In essence, as gifted and high-potential learners continue to gain a greater intrapersonal awareness, they are then better equipped to listen with understanding to the full message others share with them. This is committed listening.

I'm All Ears!

Through this activity focused on developing committed listening skills, gifted and high-potential students are placed in pairs, or, if needed, groups of three. For this simple task, one student will be directed to share a life experience (e.g., starting a new school, overcoming adversity, achieving a goal, an experience that taught them a lesson, a time they faced frustration) while the other student(s) practice committed listening. The sharing student will speak for three minutes, and the listening students are not allowed to say a word during this time. This might sound simple, but for many, it is difficult to listen without inserting words of affirmation or interjecting with a similar experience. Once the three minutes have passed, the listening student(s) will then share their "understanding" of the communicated message. What were they able to learn about the sharing student's core values (e.g., commitment, freedom, happiness, courage)? How might they be able to relate to those core values to respond in a non-judgmental manner that will lead to shared understandings? For this particular activity, it will be helpful to have a copy of Resource 4.4 available (see Chapter 4) for students to remain mindful of different core values that might be communicated through a shared experience.

The "Right" of Passage

The core of this activity is focused on active listening behaviors, meaning listening only as a means to respond. Upon completion of this activity, gifted and high-potential students will be tasked with recognizing how a sole focus on active listening often leads to a missed understanding of the shared message. Through this activity and the following reflection, gifted and high-potential learners will have a greater awareness of the committed listening that is needed for meaningful and purposeful communication.

While this activity works best with a larger group of students, it can still be used with small groups. For students to participate in this activity, they will need to sit in a circle. Sitting on the floor often works best. Each student will be given an easily picked up item (e.g., large paper clip, button, unifix cube) that they will pass to the person on either their right or their left, depending on which words they hear in the teacher read-aloud (see Table 6.8). Every time students hear a word that sounds like *right* (e.g., right, Wright, write), students will pass their item to the student on their right. Likewise, as students hear the word *left*, they will pass their item to the student sitting on their left. In essence, the students are listening to respond with the action of passing the item. It is important that the teacher continues to read the story at an appropriate pace, regardless of how successful all students are at passing the item correctly. Upon completing the read-aloud, the teacher will lead the students in a discussion focused on the reflection prompts found in Table 6.9.

Problem-Solving

When working to support gifted and high-potential learners in the goal-setting process, it is important to help them recognize the role of problem-solving within the context of effective communication and its connection to goals. First and foremost, the PEGS Model empowers students to recognize that goal setting is a way to proactively problem-solve how to achieve a desired outcome. After gaining a stronger insight into one's strengths, weaknesses, aspirations, and potential barriers (see Chapter 5), students begin to recognize the goal-setting process as a means to develop their own student agency in problem-solving to make changes that will continue to grow them in their learning and personal development.

Effective communication is key in problem-solving. As you continue to work with gifted and high-potential learners in this area, consider having them reflect on the following questions as they develop and work to achieve their goals:

- ❏ How might you best communicate with others to move forward with a solution?
- ❏ How might effective communication open up new avenues to possible solutions and flexibility of thinking?
- ❏ How do chosen words and nonverbal behaviors impact the problem-solving process in achieving a particular outcome?
- ❏ Who are key stakeholders that will be part of the problem-solving process of achieving your goal?

The following activities will continue to build effective communication skills in regard to problem-solving through a variety of situations and tasks. Continue to remain mindful of helping students make the meaningful connections between the problem-solving process, effective communication, and their personal goals.

TABLE 6.8

The Wright Family's Vacation Dilemma (Teacher Read-Aloud)

The Wright Family's Vacation Dilemma

The Wright family lived deep in the woods right at the end of a long, curving driveway to the left of a giant tree. The Wright home was very large to accommodate all the Wright family members who lived there: Papa Wright, Mama Wright, Anna Wright, John Wright, Bobby Wright, Debbie Wright, and Grandma Wright. They always did everything together because they never wanted anyone to feel left out.

One day, Mama Wright told Papa Wright, "We should take the whole Wright family on a vacation." Papa Wright quickly agreed, but when they remembered that the Wright family van was out of gas, they realized that they could only take six Wright family members with them in their smaller vehicle, and one Wright family member would have to be left behind. It was decided that Grandma Wright would be left behind.

When Grandma Wright heard the decision, she was downright angry. "Who gave you the right to not take me on the Wright family vacation," she exclaimed. "I have never left you behind, and I have raised you to make the right decisions! I always babysit Anna Wright, John Wright, Bobby Wright, and Debbie Wright, and this just isn't right that you have decided to choose me to be the one left behind! You are not in your right mind! I am going to write in my journal that I left in my room about your decision. This is not right!" At that, Grandma Wright stormed right down the hall to her bedroom on the left and slammed the door, downright angry about the situation.

The Wright family children heard Grandma Wright screaming and left their bedrooms on the left side of the hallway to go see Papa Wright and Mama Wright. "We don't want Grandma Wright to be left behind," they cried as they stood right in front of Papa Wright and Mama Wright. "This isn't right!" they exclaimed. "We have never left one of the Wright family members behind, and this is not the right decision."

Upon hearing the concerns of Anna Wright, John Wright, Bobby Wright, and Debbie Wright, Mama Wright had an idea. She turned to her left and looked Papa Wright right in his eyes. Why don't we make a Wright Family stay-cation instead, where we stay right here at the Wright family home, and we don't have to make Grandma Wright feel left out! We can take a nature hike right down by the river, make a left, turn right up the hill, and have a picnic to use up our left-overs from last night's dinner." "This is the right thing to do!" Anna Wright, John Wright, Bobby Wright, and Debbie Wright exclaimed. Papa Wright walked right down the hall to tell Grandma Wright, and she was so downright happy that she was not going to be left behind. "I knew I raised you right," Grandma Wright said to Papa Wright.

TABLE 6.9

Reflection Prompts for *The "Right" of Passage*

Reflection Prompts for *The "Right" of Passage*
• What details of the story can you remember? For example: Why, specifically, was Grandma upset beyond just being left behind? (She felt as though she had raised her son not to leave her behind, and she always babysat the Wright children, so she should be valued more.)
• What impact did those around you have on being able to understand the story that was being shared?
• How did you focus your attention on the story in regard to your response actions? How did you focus your attention on the core values of the Wright family? How does this equate to your listening behaviors in communicating to achieve a goal? How might this impact effective communication?
• Describe a time when someone might have listened to your words, but you still did not feel heard. How did that make you feel?

Does It All Add Up?

This problem-solving activity works best with a group of at least 14–16 students. To begin, students are placed into pairs and told that they will be working with their partner in a "rock, paper, scissors" style game where they will not be allowed to talk. In the same manner that "rock, paper, scissors" has partners count to three before using their hand to signify the representation of the aptly named game, students will be signifying a number of digits on one hand in the hope of achieving a total sum of 7 with their partner. They will be tasked with seeing how many times, without talking, the partnership can "throw" a sum of 7 within one minute. After sharing results of this first round, students will then be placed in groups of three, and tasked with using the same method to "throw" a sum of 11. Again, results will be shared, and the next stage includes students being placed in teams of five seeking to "throw" the sum of 21, followed by sharing their results. For the final round, students will be placed in groups of seven and tasked with "throwing" a sum of 30. For this final round, however, students will be given 30 seconds to verbally communicate with each other before starting the round. After students have been given the 30 seconds of problem-solving communication time, they are given the one-minute allotment to see how many times their group can "throw" a sum of 30. Again, results will be shared. Upon completion of this final round, engage students in reflection (see Table 6.10).

TABLE 6.10
Reflection Prompts for *Does It All Add Up?*

Reflection Prompts for *Does It All Add Up?*
• How hard was it to throw the correct sum in the first rounds of the game? How difficult was the task in the final round?
• What made "throwing" the sum of 30 easier?
• How does effective communication contribute to achieving one's goals? How might ineffective communication create additional barriers in the problem-solving process needed to achieve one's goals?
• What steps need to be in place in effective problem-solving to achieve one's goals?

It's Time for a Sit-In

Through this popular team-building activity focused on problem-solving, students stand in a perfect circle before being tasked with having everyone successfully sit on the knees of the person behind them at the same time. To achieve this task, the entire group will need to effectively communicate with one another. Upon achieving this first task, students can be further challenged by asking them to rotate the circle forward. (Special note: This can be accomplished by having everyone first take a step with their outside foot and then their inside foot, continuing forward for further rotation.) Upon completion, lead the group in a reflective discussion (see Table 6.11).

TABLE 6.11
Reflection Prompts for *It's Time for a Sit-In*

Reflection Prompts for *It's Time for a Sit-In*
• How did you feel when you first heard what the task was going to be? How does this equate to how you feel when developing a new goal?
• How important was communication in problem-solving through these tasks?
• How did effective communication create a greater sense of trust in moving forward with this task?
• How are effective communication and trust key components in problem-solving to achieve one's goals?

Linking It All Together

For this activity, students will be split into small groups that compete against each other. (Groups of five work best.) Each group will be given two to three pairs of scissors, two to three long strips of masking tape measuring 2 feet in length, and 25 sheets of scrap paper. Each group is then tasked with making the longest paper chain possible within an 8–10-minute time frame. At first, students will see this as a simple activity, until they find out that they will be sitting in a circle with their wrists tied together. (Make sure wrists are tied firmly with bandanas or string, but not so tightly that circulation is limited.) While this activity works best through this scenario, students may also be instructed to hold one hand behind their back, with only half of the team being allowed to use their dominant hand. For an additional twist, students can be further restricted by not allowing groups to speak. As students progress through the activity, continue to raise tensions by announcing in an urgent fashion how much time is remaining as every minute counts down. Upon completion of the activity and noting the length of paper chains created by each team, engage the students in a reflective discussion (see Table 6.12).

Conflict Resolution

The PEGS Model focuses on intrapersonal awareness as a primary component of goal setting. As such, gifted and high-potential students learn how

TABLE 6.12

Reflection Prompts for *Linking It All Together*

Reflection Prompts for *Linking It All Together*
• What problems did your group encounter?
• How did your group use effective communication (e.g., verbal, nonverbal) to solve these problems?
• Did seeing the other groups' actions impact how your group proceeded with the task? If so, was this fair? Why or why not?
• Did leadership or lack of leadership have an impact on the group successfully progressing with this task?
• How did announcing the amount of remaining time impact being able to achieve the given task?
• What might your group do differently if asked to repeat the task?
• How does this task relate to the process of goal setting and goal attainment?

their individual identity, values, strengths, and life experiences differ from others around them. The PEGS Model embraces diversity and recognizes that it is through our differences that our global world is able to forge new paths and embrace innovations that might never be possible.

While embracing individual differences as a strength in moving forward, there are times when individual differences might lead to conflicts of interest or differences of opinion. It is through these moments that effective communication is paramount in resolving conflict as a proactive approach to moving forward toward one's established goals. As students work toward achieving their goals, conflicts might arise between a student and another student, a student and a teacher, or a student and a parent/guardian. While there are certainly other scenarios, these constitute the majority of conflicts that gifted and high-potential students will encounter within a school setting while working to achieve a school-related goal.

As previously discussed, it is incredibly important to implement strong communication skills when resolving conflict, including verbal and nonverbal behaviors, as well as committed listening. Quite often, skills in problem-solving also come into play. Regardless of the conflict, gifted and high-potential learners should continue to practice the importance of understanding others' perspectives and remain flexible in their thinking. To further help gifted and high-potential learners understand how to navigate conflict resolution, it is important for them to also have a greater awareness of how to identify the core of the conflict itself.

Often referenced as part of collaborative practice, Rock (2008) signifies the components of SCARF (see Table 6.13) as areas that potentially threaten interactions with others, leading to conflict. Once gifted and high-potential learners are better able to understand what triggers them into feeling conflict, then they are also better equipped to effectively communicate in order to resolve conflict. For example, a gifted learner might feel conflict with a teacher when tasked with additional work upon completion of the assigned task. In this scenario, the gifted learner might feel that it is unfair that they are having to do more work than everyone else in the class. This perceived conflict with the teacher stems from the sense of *fairness* being threatened. If left unresolved, the gifted student might eventually begin underachieving as a means to avoid the extra assignments, instead of understanding the core of why they feel the lack of fairness and using that to self-advocate for differentiated work vs more work from the teacher. Table 6.13 provides a small sample of guiding questions to determine if there is a greater potential for conflict based on threats related to SCARF. An answer of "no" to any of the included questions signifies a higher potential for future conflict.

TABLE 6.13

Components of SCARF (Rock, 2008) and Connections to Potential Conflict

Component of SCARF	Guiding Questions to Determine Potential Conflict ("No" answers signify *increased* potential for conflict)
S-Status: One's perceived awareness of relation to others	• Does the gifted learner feel as though they are able to engage with intellectual or like-minded peers? • Does the gifted learner feel respected by the adult(s) in their life? • Does the gifted learner recognize their own strengths and weaknesses as well as the strengths of others?
C-Certainty: One's ability to predict the future or understand what is expected next	• Does the gifted learner have clear expectations of what is expected from them? • Does the gifted learner have a clear understanding of the purpose behind the task? • Does the gifted learner understand how the end goal is the result of smaller components and steps?
A-Autonomy: One's sense of control over events, choices, and decisions	• Does the gifted learner have choice in their learning? • Does the gifted learner have an opportunity to pursue topics of interest in their learning? • Does the gifted learner have opportunities to determine the order in which they would like to complete assigned tasks?
R-Relatedness: One's feeling of safety and connectedness with others	• Does the gifted learner have a trusted peer, teacher, or mentor? • Does the gifted learner have opportunities to find commonalities with peers? • Does the gifted learner feel as though they can approach the teacher with questions, concerns, or to self-advocate? • Does the gifted learner have a sense of connectedness with others who share similar life experiences?
F-Fairness: One's perception of the exchanges between people to be either equitable or inequitable	• Does the gifted learner have opportunities to demonstrate content mastery as a means to engage in new learning on a consistent basis? • Does the gifted learner have equitable access to learning regardless of life experiences? • Does the gifted learner have an opportunity to work through their strengths to demonstrate depth of knowledge?

The following activities provide opportunities for gifted and high-potential learners to develop stronger communication skills related to conflict resolution.

All Torn Up

This particular activity requires the use of a culmination of multiple communication skills. While it clearly involves effective verbal and nonverbal communication, it is also imperative that students listen to each other and problem-solve how to best accomplish this task. It has been included within the resolving conflict context, in large part because of the propensity this particular activity has to create conflict. Even metaphorically, it tends to represent the "torn" communication that stems from conflict.

To complete this task, students will be divided into groups of five to seven students and be given a piece of butcher paper that is 7 feet long. As groups, students will race from a starting line to a finish line (at least 20 feet away), but the trick is that all team members must stand on top of their team's butcher paper at all times. Every time the paper is torn *or* every time someone steps off the paper, a team member is blindfolded. There must always be at least one sighted person on the team at all times, so if an infraction occurs when there is no longer someone who can be blindfolded, the team must be seated for 30 seconds. Prior to beginning the race, teams should be given three minutes to discuss their strategy. The task is not complete until all teams cross the finish line. Upon completion of the race, lead students in a reflective discussion (see Table 6.14).

TABLE 6.14
Reflection Prompts for *All Torn Up*

Reflection Prompts for *All Torn Up*
• How important was the planning time? How do you equate this to the time needed to create purposeful goals?
• In what ways did you have to adjust the plan during the activity? How might this relate to working toward your goals?
• How did you feel when you were responsible for an infraction? How did you feel when others were responsible for an infraction?
• How important was communication in successfully navigating this task? Why?
• Throughout the activity which components of SCARF, if any, triggered you into feelings of conflict with others on your team? How did you work to resolve those feelings to be able to finish the task? How might this equate to resolving conflict in relation to achieving your goals?

Conflict Resolution Spiral

Nobody likes conflict, but it is important for all students to learn how to effectively communicate to resolve any conflict that might arise in their daily lives and, even more importantly, while working to achieve their goals. Due to the personal nature of conflict and how it threatens us through the different components of SCARF (see Table 6.13), students often need a process to learn how to navigate conflict resolution. For this purpose, we would like to introduce the Conflict Resolution Spiral (see Figure 6.2).

As part of the Conflict Resolution Spiral, gifted and high-potential learners work through a process to learn how to navigate the often-delicate waters of communication. With conflict resolution being very personal in nature, this activity is most beneficial when an individual is able to process this information with a trusted teacher, mentor, or parent. The steps proceed in the following manner:

1. **Identify the conflict:** At this stage, an individual identifies the conflict and the people involved.
2. **Identify the feelings you are having because of the conflict:** An individual needs to be able to articulate their feelings stemming from the

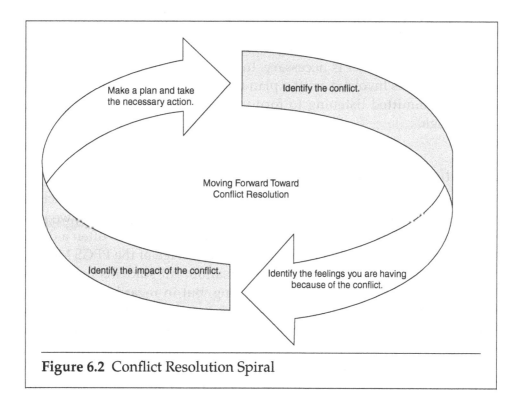

Figure 6.2 Conflict Resolution Spiral

conflict (e.g., powerless, unseen, taken advantage of, scared). In conjunction with identifying the feelings stemming from the conflict, the individual should also connect which component of SCARF is being threatened by this conflict (e.g., status, certainty, autonomy, relatedness, fairness). In doing so, the student is better equipped to be proactive in resolving the conflict in a nonthreatening manner.

3. **Identify the impact of the conflict:** It is important to identify the impact of the conflict because the level of impact determines the degree of priority placed on resolving that conflict. After all, there are differing degrees of conflict based on how significantly the conflict impacts an individual's life. For the purposes of goal attainment, gifted and high-potential students should be mindful of being proactive in resolving conflict that could potentially impede their progress to achieving their goals (e.g., misunderstanding with a teacher, lack of collaboration with peer group, restricted access to materials by an individual). Upon reflection with a student, there might be times when it is determined the conflict is not worth the time, energy, and resources required to pursue it any further. This is often the case in situations that are beyond a student's control or are conflicts that are more surface level and do not impact goal attainment and/or have a measurable impact on an individual's life.

4. **Make a plan and take the necessary action:** For areas of conflict that *do* have an impact on an individual's daily life and impede the ability to achieve their goals, making a plan and taking necessary action to resolve the conflict is necessary. In this stage, students identify the stakeholders involved, craft a plan for integrating proactive dialogue and committed listening to formulate a solution, and then follow through.

Adapting to New Situations

One of the few "constants" in life is to expect the unexpected. In fact, it often seems that no matter how much time, effort, and planning we put into something, inevitably, the unexpected happens. This is often a difficult life lesson to learn, but through the second stage of the PEGS Model, this is explicitly brought into the conversation. All students need to be aware of adaptability and flexible thinking, but in regard to gifted and high-potential learners, their acute awareness and heightened sense of fairness (Sisk, 2021) can often derail them when unexpected events occur.

One way that teachers of the gifted can begin this conversation is by sharing personal experiences about having to adapt to and overcome unforeseen challenges (e.g., Covid-19 pandemic, bad weather canceling outdoor plans, unexpected illness). While it is often easier to commiserate with others about negative outcomes, the PEGS Model focuses gifted and high-potential learners on the positive outcomes that stem from effective communication. With this focus students begin to leverage their adaptability, flexibility, and resiliency. As with many interpersonal skills, adapting to new situations requires choosing appropriate words and actions in addition to problem-solving and, quite often, conflict resolution. The following activities provide opportunities for students to "adapt" to unforeseen situations. Through these experiences and subsequent reflections, gifted and high-potential students begin to make connections back to their own goals. In return, they are able to exercise flexibility of thinking from the onset of goal design.

A Recipe for Successful Change

The simple act of anticipating change can often elicit additional feelings of anxiety in gifted and high-potential learners (Peterson, 2008). When working with this population of students, begin by asking, "On a scale from 1 to 10, how confident do you feel in your interpersonal (communication) skills to successfully navigate change?" and "On a scale of 1 to 10, how would you rate your feelings of anxiety in regard to navigating substantial changes in your life, with 1 being the lowest level of anxiety and 10 being the highest?" From the conversations that stem from these two questions, have students reflect back on what they learned about themselves through the first stage of PEGS: Know Thyself. Have them make a list of their strengths, core values, and natural talents (see Chapter 4; Resource 4.5).

Once students have completed their lists, let them know they will be creating A Recipe for Successful Change using their strengths as the ingredients. As part of the recipe, students will need to remain mindful of their own intrapersonal awareness and ability to communicate effectively through change, while also leveraging their personal strengths to overcome any potential barriers. Table 6.15 provides a sample recipe for successful change.

Moving in New Directions

Without a doubt, it is beneficial for gifted and high-potential learners to remain mindful of the desired outcomes they are working toward. With

TABLE 6.15

A Recipe for Successful Change (Sample)

Recipe for Successful Change
Bounce-Back Bread

Ingredients:

2 cups of commitment	1 ½ cups of knowledge
1 cup of resilience	¼ cup of independence
2 Tbsp creativity	A pinch of choleric seasoning

1. First, gently combine the two primary ingredients: commitment and knowledge. The strength of these two ingredients will provide a strong base for the final dish. Do not overmix, as each of these two flavors can be weakened if not treated with respect.

2. Allow at least 1 hour for this mixture to solidify before adding any of the remaining ingredients. This will allow for a greater consistency in moving forward.

3. Once commitment and knowledge have had time to rest, add resiliency and independence to the mixture. Upon adding these ingredients, expect to see a stronger consistency begin to take shape. This will continue to strengthen the mixture into a dough-like form.

4. Carefully knead the dough, being mindful that all components need to work together. It might be helpful to bring in an extra set of hands to help in this process. Once the dough has been worked together, allow the dough to rest in preparation for the next steps.

5. Once the dough is reflective in texture, gently add the final ingredients of creativity and a pinch of choleric seasoning. These final ingredients add a little extra flavoring and durability to the dish.

6. Allow the dough to bake at 350°F until it springs back from a gentle push.

7. Cool until ready to serve and enjoy the effort you put into creating the dish.

8. Share the dish and your baking experience with others.

---

this being said, it is equally important that they recognize this path is not always a straight one. Throughout the goal-attainment process, there are often unexpected twists, turns, and obstacles that must be navigated in order to achieve the desired outcomes. In short, it is important that students do not have tunnel vision while working to achieve goals. To support gifted and high-potential students in this process, the following activity provides a physical activity that represents the concept of adaptability in thinking.

This activity can be used one-on-one, in a small group, or whole class. To begin, the teacher stands in front of the participating students and asks students to mirror four simple actions: arms extended above head, arms extended down toward feet, arms extended to the left, arms extended to the right. As students mirror the teacher's actions, the students will need to say aloud the designated action. For example, as students mimic arms extended above the head, they will say, "Above." In terms of the left and right mirrored actions, the students will be stating their direction, not the direction of the teacher (i.e., the teacher's left will be the students' right). Make sure that students feel comfortable with these directions before proceeding to the following rounds.

Once students are successful at mimicking the motion and verbalizing the direction (e.g., above, down, left, right), the students will face new adaptations of this game through the following scenarios:

❏ Students move arms in the same direction as the teacher, but state the opposite direction. For example, students will move arms up as they say, "Down."

❏ Students say the motion they see from the teacher but move in the opposite direction. For example, if the teacher moves their arms down, then the students will say, "Down," but extend their arms above their heads.

After playing this game for several rounds, begin to have students sit down once they miss an action/word. As the game continues, increase the speed to which the actions are given to increase the difficulty associated with the task.

While this activity is not directly tied to the act of effective communication, per se, it does present students with the often uncomfortable feeling associated with having to adapt their thinking or adjust actions that might not come naturally. It is through the reflection of this activity (see Table 6.16) that gifted and high-potential learners are better able to understand and connect to the flexibility of thought that often coincides with adapting to new situations.

Additional Tools for Developing Interpersonal Skills

In addition to the specific resources listed above, there are a variety of additional tools that continue to support students in developing interpersonal skills. These can take the form of role play scenarios, such as taking on the persona of someone working through conflict resolution, practicing how to react to nonverbal communication appropriately, or role playing through different self-advocacy scenarios. It is also powerful to have opportunities for gifted and high-potential learners to share personal stories about problem-solving, adapting to new situations, and resolving

TABLE 6.16

Reflection Prompts for *Moving in New Directions*

Reflection Prompts for *Moving in New Directions*
• What made this game difficult?
• How does this equate to how you might feel when faced with an unexpected situation?
• How important is it for our words and actions to work together when working to achieve our goals?
• Did the addition of having to sit out add any additional pressure to the game? What outside stressors might impact how you adapt to new, unexpected situations?
• When we set goals, it is easy to have tunnel vision in working to achieve those goals. Why is it important to be flexible and adaptable while working toward goal attainment?

conflict and reflecting upon how effective communication played an integral part in successful outcomes. This requires a trusting and respectful environment, but is incredibly powerful in creating relatedness among gifted and high-potential learners.

Because of the emphasis on verbal communication skills within interpersonal awareness, it is also important that scaffolds are in place to support multilingual learners, twice-exceptional learners, and gifted and high-potential students who might be lacking in confidence in this area. Developing effective communication can often feel intimidating, so providing sentence stems, visuals, and offering clarification, redirection, and reflection of learning in a nonthreatening, inclusive environment is paramount in this process.

In addition to the various scaffolds to further support gifted and high-potential learners in the development of effective communication, Resource 6.1 provides a template to guide students in reflecting upon how their intrapersonal awareness (see Chapter 5) continues to contribute to the interpersonal skills that are explored in this stage of PEGS: Express Thyself. Together, the intrapersonal and interpersonal awareness continue to contribute to the creation of personal, purposeful, and empowering goals for each student. By working through this resource, gifted and high-potential learners are better prepared to communicate their needs as related to their goal. This continues to increase their interpersonal awareness while being proactive in moving forward toward goal attainment.

RESOURCE 6.1
Effective Communication Toward Goal Development

Name: _____

Intrapersonal Awareness for Goal Development
• *What have you learned about yourself that might contribute to the development of your goal?*
• *What do you know about yourself that might help you work through a potential barrier?*

Use what you know about your strengths, values, and natural talents to make connections to your interpersonal, communication skills in the Personal Insights column.	
Questions to Consider	**Personal Insights**
Verbal/Nonverbal Communication Skills *Who are the key stakeholders you might need to communicate with while working toward your goal?* *How does your intrapersonal awareness (e.g., values, strengths, natural talents) contribute to how you communicate (e.g., verbal, nonverbal) with others while working toward your goal?* *In what ways might you use Presuming Positive Intent within your communication with others while working to achieve your goal?*	
Committed Listening *How does your understanding of core values contribute to the committed listening necessary to achieve your goal?* *How does committed listening provide insight to how you move forward with your verbal communication?*	

Problem-Solving/Conflict Resolution/Adapting *How might you remain solutions-focused within your communications while working toward your goal?* *In what ways might you use your strengths while communicating to problem-solve, resolve conflict, and adapt to unexpected events?* *How might you remain flexible in your interpersonal skills while working to achieve your goal?*	
Reflection: *How do these insights provide a greater awareness of where you are and where you want to go?*	

Interpersonal and Intrapersonal Reflection

While this chapter has been focused on the interpersonal awareness needed for gifted and high-potential learners to effectively communicate their needs in regard to student-driven goals, it is also important to remain mindful of the closely related intrapersonal awareness discussed in Chapter 5. The PEGS Model is highly intertwined, and as such, it is integral that gifted and high-potential learners recognize how the stages of PEGS support and build upon each other. For example, in the case of interpersonal communication skills, gifted and high-potential learners should continue to leverage their personal strengths, awareness of core values, and natural talents as they work to communicate with others toward achieving their goals. Key questions to guide students in this thinking might include:

❏ What have I learned about my own interpersonal communication skills in regard to achieving my goal?
❏ How might I use my strengths as I communicate my needs with others?
❏ How do my intrapersonal awareness and interpersonal skills support me in self-advocacy efforts?

Once these core intrapersonal and interpersonal skills are explored in tandem, the next stage of PEGS will guide gifted and high-potential students in making connections to how their goals are aligned and applied to the learning process.

References

Bohm, B. (1996). *On dialogue*. Routledge.

Gagné, F. (2021). *Differentiating giftedness from talent: The DMGT perspective on talent development*. Routledge.

Kee, K., Anderson, K., Dearing, V., Harris, E., & Shuster, F. (2010). *Results coaching: The new essentials for school leaders*. Corwin.

Mofield, E., & Phelps, V. (in press). *Coaching in gifted education*. Routledge.

Peterson, J. S. (2008). *The essential guide to talking with gifted teens: Ready-to-use discussions about identity, relationships, and more*. Free Spirit Publishing.

Rock, D. (2008). SCARF: A brain-based model for collaborating with and influencing others. *NeuroLeadership Journal, 1*, 78–87.

Sisk, D. (2021). Managing the emotional intensities of gifted students with mindfulness practices. *Educational Sciences, 11*, 1–12. https://doi.org/10.3390/educsci11110731

CHAPTER 7

Apply Thyself

The Third Stage of Goal Development

At its core, the PEGS Model is founded on empowering gifted and high-potential students through goal setting that will have a positive impact on their learning. While this is most often associated with goals that support students in progressing within a school setting, goals do not have to be based solely on academic achievement. Depending on each student's needs and aspirations, they may choose to focus a goal on academic achievement, or they might elect to focus on other skills that continue to move them forward in developing their sense of self as a learner. These additional areas might include, but are not limited to, developing goals focused on improving collaborative practice, exploring creative outlets, developing social relationships, or growing leadership opportunities. Regardless of the area of focus, the third stage of PEGS, Apply Thyself, continues to support gifted and high-potential learners in the next step of crafting their goals. More specifically, students will begin to craft how their goals will be applied to the learning process and identify how they will measure their progress along the way.

DOI: 10.4324/9781003331049-8

The Power of the Path

As discussed in Chapter 1, Gagné's (2021) Differentiating Model of Giftedness and Talent (DMGT; see Figure 7.1) recognizes how gifted and high-potential learners' ability to demonstrate their talents is impacted by their intrapersonal awareness (e.g., needs, values, goal setting, autonomy, determination), interpersonal skills (e.g., social constructs, interpersonal relationships), and the developmental process (e.g., access, investment, progress). While we continue to make these connections clear throughout the book, this understanding becomes even more significant in the third stage of PEGS for a variety of reasons, the first being communicated through the visual representation of the DMGT, itself.

Gagné's (2021) DMGT visually depicts the developmental process as being the *only* component within the model that is impacted by a student's aptitudes, as well as by both the environmental and intrapersonal components. In addition, the developmental process is also the *only* route, or pathway, through which a student is enabled to demonstrate their levels of learning, depth of understanding, and subsequent competencies in relation to their talents.

Due to the impact of the developmental process on a student's ability to not only apply, but also demonstrate their degree of content mastery or level of goal achievement, this third stage of PEGS targets application to the learning process. With this focus, gifted and high-potential students feel more empowered to work toward their goals because they also recognize the purpose behind the goal (Phelps, 2022). The PEGS Model provides the structure to guide students in this process.

As gifted and high-potential learners begin to recognize how to "apply" themselves through PEGS, it also becomes necessary to understand the various considerations that impact the developmental process as outlined in the DMGT. Gagné (2021) divides this component into three categories: activities, investment, and progress. Each of these categories are key within the goal development process and as such become key factors in the PEGS Model.

Apply Thyself: Activities

While the DMGT's developmental process serves as the pathway for gifted and high-potential learners to demonstrate their progress and ultimate achievement of their goals, the activities category provides three distinct considerations in regard to goal setting. Gagné (2021) outlines these as

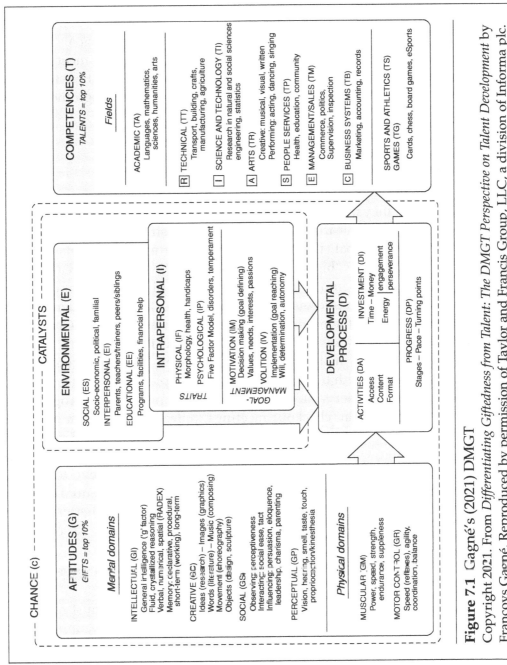

Figure 7.1 Gagné's (2021) DMGT

Copyright 2021. From *Differentiating Giftedness from Talent: The DMGT Perspective on Talent Development* by Françoys Gagné. Reproduced by permission of Taylor and Francis Group, LLC, a division of Informa plc.

content, access, and format. By working through each of these factors, gifted and high-potential learners begin to further craft and refine their personalized goals.

After working through the first two stages of PEGS, students generally have a fairly strong idea of what they would like their goals to focus on. With this in mind, they must now begin to address what meeting their goals will "look" like, how progress will be monitored, and how they will assess if their goals have been achieved. By working through the lens of content, access, and format, there is greater clarity of how a goal can be carefully crafted to have the most impact.

Content

As gifted and high-potential students focus more intently on the content of their goal, they first consider how the topic, itself, can be applied within their progression of learning. Then they explore strategies that might help them reach their goal. This is often difficult for gifted students because they quickly see the "big picture," but often have difficulty breaking the "big picture" down into smaller, more strategic pieces that support them in achieving the desired outcome. For example, a gifted student might recognize through their gained intrapersonal awareness (see Chapter 5) that they need to work on completing and turning in assignments on time. Recognizing this as an area for growth, however, does not automatically provide students with the strategies (e.g., use a planner, use a technology reminder app, folder systems, accountability partner) or progression points (e.g., check-in/checkout meetings, reflections, focus on one content area before adding more) needed to improve in this area, nor does it acknowledge what barriers (e.g., extracurriculars, video games, social media) might need to be addressed to successfully achieve this goal. During this stage of goal development, gifted and high-potential learners systematically consider these different components to further craft their goals to be purposeful, explicit, measurable, and attainable. Resource 7.1 provides a structure for working through this process.

Access

Once the content of the goal is in greater focus, students must now consider the concept of access in regard to their goal. For example, if an artistic student sets a goal to become more involved in the school's theater program as a means to develop leadership in this area, there are several access issues that need to be considered. First, is there an already established procedure in place that all students must first successfully audition to be admitted to the school's theater program? Second, does the school's theater program require after-school meeting times and subsequent transportation to participate? Finally, is there a financial obligation to participate in this program (e.g., costumes, stage make-up, dues) that might inhibit this student's ability to participate? If so, are there any options for financial assistance?

Lack of access can often be disheartening but, unfortunately, it is a real consideration in terms of setting goals. By no means does this signify that lack of access means that a goal is not attainable, it simply raises awareness of potential barriers that need to be addressed as an area for proactive problem-solving and a means to identify points of contact. Resource 7.1 continues to help students note these various considerations.

Format

As gifted and high-potential students continue to complete Resource 7.1, they will also begin to refine their goals by synthesizing their goals' Content Considerations and Access and Accessibility information. It is important to note that there might be instances as students complete the *Goal Development Pathway* where they recognize how the lack of access might currently inhibit them from pursuing a particular goal. Again, this does not mean the goal cannot be pursued and ultimately achieved; it just means that more time needs to be given to exploring the potential barriers and proactively problem-solving and/or advocating for new procedures within that area. In these instances, the goal might actually evolve into exploring these options as a means to elicit change. There are other times, however, when the student might be equally as interested in pursuing another goal and ultimately decide to work toward a different goal. Be respectful and supportive of these decisions, as this process continues to develop student agency within the goal-setting process.

RESOURCE 7.1
Goal Development Pathway

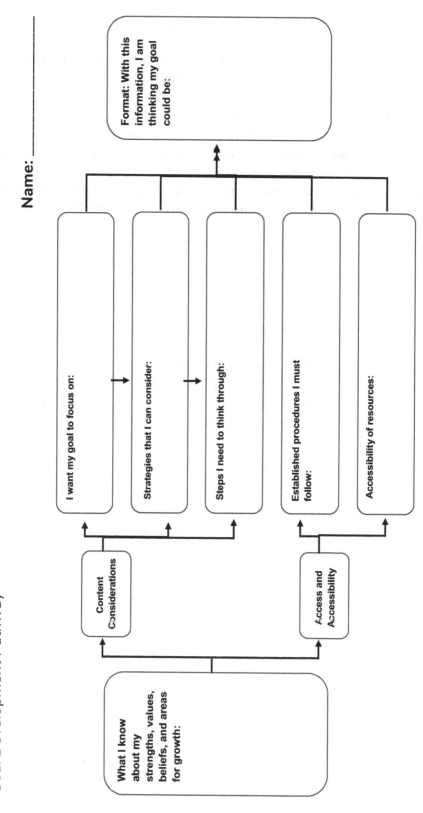

Name: _____

Format: With this information, I am thinking my goal could be:

I want my goal to focus on:

Strategies that I can consider:

Steps I need to think through:

Established procedures I must follow:

Accessibility of resources:

Content Considerations

Access and Accessibility

What I know about my strengths, values, beliefs, and areas for growth:

Apply Thyself: Investment

Once gifted and high-potential students have thoughtfully worked through the content, access, and format considerations of their goals, it is equally important for them to recognize their own personal investment in their goals. This step is highly representative of the Apply Thyself stage of PEGS, as students truly begin to evaluate the degree of commitment they have in regard to their goals. This will be measured through the time, engagement, and perseverance they are willing to commit to achieving their goals.

When working through this phase with gifted and high-potential learners, it might be beneficial to guide students in creating metaphorical connections related to the word, *investment*. This can be accomplished by simply asking, "What do you think of when you hear the word, investment?" Most students will quickly equate investments to money by referencing the stock market, savings accounts, or real estate investments. Continue to challenge students to think of investments that are focused on the key attributes of time, engagement, and perseverance. With a little prompting, students might reference that individuals can also make investments in themselves by pursuing degrees in higher education, eating healthy diets and exercising, training for the Olympics, or even learning a new language. Each of these investments in one's self require an individual to put forth effort, perseverance, and remain committed to the end goal.

As the PEGS Model consistently seeks to develop student agency, it is important that the goals developed through this process are purposeful and meaningful, which in turn continues to help gifted and high-potential learners recognize the value in the goals they have created. In this latter stage of goal development, it is often worthwhile for gifted and high-potential learners to complete a *Personal Investment Pledge* (see Resource 7.2). This pledge serves two purposes:

1. To help each student explicitly make connections to the purpose, value, and future impact of their self-selected goal.
2. To provide a formative assessment measure to gain a greater insight into how each student is connecting with their developing goal.

If a student is unable to complete the *Personal Investment Pledge*, then it is possible that the goal might need further revision to better align with the student's intrapersonal needs and strengths.

RESOURCE 7.2
Personal Investment Pledge

Name: _____

My Goal: (Write your developing goal in this section.)
Complete the following statements:
Reasons why this goal is an investment in myself:
This will help me in my future by:
Because I am worth this investment, I plan to dedicate time to achieving this goal in the following manner:
I understand that meaningful goals often encounter obstacles. If this happens while I am working to achieve this goal, I will:
Others will know that I am invested in working to achieve this goal by seeing me:

Apply Thyself: Progress

The final stage of PEGS: Apply Thyself guides gifted and high-potential learners through the process of examining how they will self-assess progress toward their goals. What are the time parameters they would like to accomplish the goal in? Which steps of their goals might take more time than others? What type of pace do they want to set for themselves? These are all key considerations as students continue to refine their goals.

As teachers and mentors work with gifted and high-potential learners throughout this final stage, it is important they remain mindful of several factors that often emerge during this phase of goal setting. Gagné (2021) stresses the importance of recognizing different perspectives in regard to the connotation of the word, progression. Take the time to talk about this with your students. Ask them what progression means to them and how they will be able to measure this progression toward their goals. For this discussion, it might be helpful to remind students of their work on the *Goal Development Pathway* (see Resource 7.1). As students recognize and develop the steps needed to achieve their goals, this also outlines check-in opportunities for reflection and self-assessment of progress toward their goals.

Some goals are easily measured by quantitative data related to their desired outcomes (e.g., attendance, grades, accumulated points). Other goals require more qualitative means to assess progress. For example, students might keep reflection logs that reference their current levels of motivation, positive inner dialogue, or higher degrees of patience. Resource 7.3 serves as an additional self-assessment tool to empower students in this process.

Aligned with the NAGC (2019) Gifted Education Programming Standards, the *Student Self-Assessment of Progress* is beneficial to use at the onset of the PEGS program and at various times throughout the year as a means for gifted and high-potential learners to recognize their own growth within goal setting and their developing student agency.

As an additional note, make it clear to students that goals are not set in stone. Quite often, as gifted and high-potential learners continue to grow, learn, and evolve, goals need to be revised and modified based on new information, unexpected events, or various other factors that impact goal attainment. Gagné (2021) refers to these as "turning points," and they provide an opportunity for students to reconnect with a purposeful goal when needed.

RESOURCE 7.3
Student Self-Assessment of Progress

Name: _____

I understand how my interests, strengths, and needs guide my goal-related decisions.

1	2	3	4	5	6	7	8	9	10
Strongly Disagree									Strongly Agree

Reflective Insights:

I understand how my identity, culture, beliefs, and values guide my goal-related decisions.

1	2	3	4	5	6	7	8	9	10
Strongly Disagree									Strongly Agree

Reflective Insights:

I determine the resources needed to accomplish my goals.

1	2	3	4	5	6	7	8	9	10
Strongly Disagree									Strongly Agree

Reflective Insights:

I frequently self-assess my progress while working to achieve my goals.

1	2	3	4	5	6	7	8	9	10
Strongly Disagree									Strongly Agree

Reflective Insights:

I articulate how my awareness and abilities in goal setting have grown and evolved.

1	2	3	4	5	6	7	8	9	10
Strongly Disagree									Strongly Agree

Reflective Insights:

I understand how my goals connect with the real world.									
1 Strongly Disagree	2	3	4	5	6	7	8	9	10 Strongly Agree

Reflective Insights:

I independently develop and achieve purposeful goals.									
1 Strongly Disagree	2	3	4	5	6	7	8	9	10 Strongly Agree

Reflective Insights:

I feel confident in self-advocating for my needs.									
1 Strongly Disagree	2	3	4	5	6	7	8	9	10 Strongly Agree

Reflective Insights:

I feel confident in my goal-related abilities.									
1 Strongly Disagree	2	3	4	5	6	7	8	9	10 Strongly Agree

Reflective Insights:

I feel confident in my ability to effectively communicate with others.									
1 Strongly Disagree	2	3	4	5	6	7	8	9	10 Strongly Agree

Reflective Insights:

I adapt and problem-solve while working to achieve my goal.									
1 Strongly Disagree	2	3	4	5	6	7	8	9	10 Strongly Agree

Reflective Insights:

Created by V. Phelps and K. Lewis as adapted from NAGC (2019) Gifted Programing Standards.

Celebrate Success

One of the greatest gifts we can give our students is the ability to celebrate their success. This does not mean focusing on the final product of goal attainment. To the contrary, it means celebrating the *process* of working through all of the steps needed to arrive at the end goal. As the PEGS Model continues to stress reflective practice, metacognitive mindfulness, and respect for oneself and others, celebrate with students and recognize even the smallest of accomplishments. Even when a strength-based approach is taken, working toward goals can often present gifted and high-potential students with having to address areas that might not come easily to them. This is powerful. This is purposeful. This is igniting potential.

In addition to scheduling times to touch base with each student to monitor how they are progressing toward their goal, consider having students create a portfolio of the various planning documents, activities, reflections, work samples, and various artifacts that represent their work in goal setting. Make sure that all portfolio items are dated and, as appropriate, encourage students to include any additional insights through short reflections within the portfolios. Over the course of time, these portfolios serve as a great source of evidence for gifted and high-potential students to truly recognize their progress, not only in regard to their goals, but also in terms of growing in self-awareness, reflective practice, and resiliency. All too often, gifted and high-potential learners are eager to see significant changes in a short period of time, which isn't always possible or practical. Portfolios serve as a reminder that progress, no matter how fast or slow, is something to be celebrated. After all, Rome wasn't built in a day!

References

Gagné, F. (2021). *Differentiating giftedness from talent: The DMGT perspective on talent development*. Routledge.

National Association for Gifted Children. (2019). *2019 Pre-K–Grade 12 Gifted Programming Standards*. www.nagc.org/sites/default/files/standards/Intro%202019%20Programming%20Standards.pdf

Phelps, V. (2022). Motivating gifted adolescents through the power of PIE: Preparedness, innovation, and effort. *Roeper Review*, 44(1), 35–48. https://doi.10.1080/02783193.2021.2005204

CHAPTER 8

Implementing Purposeful Empowerment in Goal Setting

With the foundations of Purposeful Empowerment in Goal Setting (PEGS) now securely established, the process of how to implement this strength-based goal-setting model will be reviewed. In this chapter, teachers will find how the process is used with students and resources for having purposeful goal-setting meetings. Specific needs of students in the middle grades will be highlighted, and examples of implementation will show how this process has been successfully used with gifted and high-potential learners.

PEGS and Middle Grade Students

The beginning of adolescence can be a very tumultuous time for a gifted or high-potential learner. Their brain is beginning to make more sense of the world while their body is changing at a rapid rate. Asynchronous development may increase their intelligence, yet other areas of their brain development may be lacking (Cavilla, 2019; Souza, 2009). Gifted and high-potential students may have an increased awareness about current events, their own inner world, and peer relationships. Students in the middle grades are also asked to achieve at high levels in more rigorous classes and with increased autonomy. They may have difficulty navigating this

DOI: 10.4324/9781003331049-9

new world because their brains are developing at a rapid rate and pruning away connections that are no longer needed (Siegel & Payne Bryson, 2012). This could possibly cause issues in areas like decision-making, impulse control, and planning for what should happen next.

Gifted and high-potential students also begin to become more critical of themselves and their work. They hold themselves to high standards and begin to judge others as well. With new awareness of the world, these students may begin to develop maladaptive habits in procrastination and underachievement. The PEGS Model provides the needed tools to combat these negative effects. PEGS gives the students a lens for viewing what is going on within themselves so they can see the real picture.

Specific Needs of Middle Schoolers

Gifted and high-potential learners need to be shown how to set and achieve goals, keep going when it becomes challenging, and be ok with challenges and failures (Rakow, 2020). These are skills that many teachers and parents think they should already have by the middle grades. However, these are not always innate. Middle grade students also need to have instruction on how to plan and follow through with assignments, along with developing and using organization and time management skills. Gifted and high-potential students also have the ability to under-stand abstract concepts and should have opportunities to explore these through many different perspectives. They need guidance on how to process serious world and local events. They must have strategies to work through their intense emotions. The PEGS Model provides supports for gifted and high-potential students to address these needs through a strength-based approach.

How to Implement PEGS with Gifted and High-Potential Students

The PEGS Model is designed to guide gifted and high-potential students in their goal setting. To implement this model, it is important for the teacher to have a regularly scheduled time to talk with the student about the PEGS process. Whether PEGS is implemented with a whole group or an indi-vidual student, it is imperative that these meetings, or conferences, be one-on-one and confidential. During these scheduled meetings, students may uncover things about themselves that are uncomfortable to discuss. They may also encounter issues and need a safe person to confide in. Students need a trusted adult to respect their thoughts, be direct, and give them a realistic view of what is happening (Rakow, 2020).

Though the PEGS Model is set up as a one-on-one strategy, it can be used in other ways. The teacher could use the assessments and interventions (see Chapters 4–6) with an entire class or small group. The teacher would then schedule times to conference with the students individually on their specific goals and needs. The PEGS Model could also be used as a peer-to-peer model, with the students acting as the trusted mentor. Having gifted and high-potential students act as a mentor for their peers can aid in the development of leadership skills. If a teacher implements this process as a peer-to-peer model, it is important to begin with discussing respect and trust with students. It may be difficult for some students to open up to others. The teacher must develop a compassionate and trusting environment in order for students to collaborate respectfully. Pairing older students with younger students would be recommended with this use. Older students will have gained experience and insight into some of the areas that they can share with younger peers. Teachers should act as the facilitator in this method, providing direction, guidance, and assistance as necessary. Whether PEGS is used as a one-on-one session with the teacher, a whole group intervention with teacher–student conferencing, or as a peer-to-peer goal-setting method, it is a useful tool in empowering students to take charge of their learning. An overview of the options for implementation is shown in Table 8.1.

Who Can Benefit from PEGS?

Research and best practices have shown that gifted learners can benefit from instruction on how to recognize their strengths and barriers and then set goals accordingly (Wehmeyer, 2002). Purposeful Empowerment in Goal Setting has been designed to provide that instruction. However, it may not be realistic for a teacher to use the one-on-one method for every student. In that case, teachers should provide this service for students who are most in need. To determine this, a teacher must work with the school team to gather information and data to understand the learner's specific needs. When the school team agrees the student is in need of instruction or intervention in these areas, services can be added to the student's educational plan, or time can be set aside during the student's classes. The school team can utilize the Student Needs Checklist (see Resource 8.1) as a guide for understanding specific areas the learner may be struggling in.

TABLE 8.1

Options for Implementing PEGS with Students

One-on-One Teacher–Student Method	Whole Group Method with Teacher–Student Conferences	Peer-to-Peer Method with Teacher Facilitation
• Student takes assessments individually • Teacher regularly conferences with student about results • Teacher and student discuss barriers and set goals • Teacher provides the student with opportunities to reflect on progress regularly	• Students take assessments as a whole group • Teacher regularly conferences with students individually • Teacher and students discuss barriers and set goals • Teacher administers interventions to whole group • Teacher provides students with opportunities to reflect on progress regularly	• Students take assessments as a whole group • Students are paired, and teacher builds a respectful, trusting environment • Students regularly conference with their partner • Students discuss barriers and set goals • Teacher provides interventions as necessary • Students have opportunities to reflect on progress regularly

This checklist can also be helpful in deciding what assessments to give at the beginning of the PEGS process. Students who are twice-exceptional or from typically underrepresented groups can greatly benefit from PEGS, and this should be noted on the checklist as well. Once the teacher has established a regular time to meet with the student, the PEGS process can begin with building the respectful, trusting relationship between teacher and student.

RESOURCE 8.1
Student Needs Checklist

Name: _____

Intrapersonal Awareness

Needs in the following areas extend beyond that of their gifted peers:

- ☐ Recognizing own strengths
- ☐ Recognizing own weaknesses
- ☐ Time management
- ☐ Confidence
- ☐ Anxiety
- ☐ Autonomy (self-directed learner)
- ☐ Effort
- ☐ Perseverance
- ☐ Accountability
- ☐ Resilience

Interpersonal Awareness

Needs in the following areas extend beyond that of their gifted peers:

- ☐ Leadership
- ☐ Active listening
- ☐ Effective communication
- ☐ Adaptability
- ☐ Advocacy (Expressing one's needs)
- ☐ Resolving conflict
- ☐ Problem-solving with peers, teachers, parents, and mentors

Learning Process

Needs in the following areas extend beyond that of their gifted peers:

- ☐ Underachievement
- ☐ Unhealthy perfectionism
- ☐ Accountability

Other extenuating circumstances that might impact any of the above areas:

_____

_____

_____

_____

Fostering a Respectful Relationship

As a gifted student peels back the layers of themselves to reveal their underlying thoughts, values, and beliefs, they may encounter things that are not easy to talk about. Students may feel shame or inadequacy as they talk about barriers they have within themselves, in their communication, and/or in their education. If they are to speak openly and fully about their struggles, they must have a relationship with their partner that is nonjudgmental and respectful. The person they reveal these things to must be trustworthy and able to give honest feedback to the student.

Whether the student is partnered with a classmate or a teacher for PEGS, it is important to first discuss the rules of the session. The teacher must pledge to respect the student's thoughts and ideas and to not reveal confidential information to others. However, any information shared with the teacher will be divulged to necessary stakeholders if that information alludes to the physical harm of someone. With this being said, if the student reveals that they are thinking about self-harm, suicide, harming others, or are visibly under the influence, this information should be given to the school administration, school counselors, and/or other emergency organizations. The teacher should also pledge to give the student direct and appropriate feedback while using respectful communication.

The student should pledge to be open and honest about their thoughts, ideas, and behaviors. They should pledge to be respectful to the teacher and have an open mind toward the feedback given. The student should also agree to follow through with the goals set to the best of their ability. Table 8.2 shows the pledges between teacher and student. If the PEGS process is used in a peer-to-peer method, the students should either assume the teacher role or the student role and abide by the pledges as well. It is important in the peer-to-peer method that the teacher monitors the interactions between students and guides them as necessary.

Analyzing Student Abilities

The next step in implementing PEGS is for the teacher to administer the intrapersonal and interpersonal assessments with gifted and high-potential students (see Chapter 4). These assessments help students recognize their giftedness and creativity traits, their social aptitudes, and their temperament and personality, along with their resiliency, core values, motivations, and volition. As previously discussed, the teacher can use the results from the Student Needs Checklist (see Resource 8.1) to drive

TABLE 8.2
PEGS Teacher and Student Pledge

As the teacher, I pledge:	As the student, I pledge:
• To respect your thoughts and opinions.	• To be open and honest about my thoughts, ideas, and behaviors.
• To not reveal confidential information to anyone outside our meetings unless it could be harmful to someone.	• To be respectful in my communication with you.
• To give you direct and appropriate feedback.	• To be open minded toward your feedback and guidance.
• To be respectful in my communication with you.	• To follow through with the goals we set to the best of my ability.

which assessments are important based on students' needs. If the teacher is unsure which assessments should be used, it is recommended to assess the student's personality, resilience, core values, and psychosocial skills.

Using these assessments, gifted and high-potential students create a snapshot of themselves that will inform the Assessments Analysis (see Resource 5.1). As students complete the assessments and have conversations with the teacher to reflect on them, they should record the results in the correct category in Resource 5.1: Strengths and Barriers, Personality Traits, Core Values, Attitudes, and Motivations. This analysis grid will act as the student's strengths log throughout the entire PEGS process. This should be kept in a folder, binder section, or other safe place, along with the other PEGS materials, so students can refer back to it to remind themselves of their strengths. They will use these strengths as a lens through which they will analyze barriers and problem-solve to set goals.

Using PEGS Resources as Interventions

When the student has completed the intrapersonal and interpersonal assessments and the Assessments Analysis, the teacher and student begin to set goals to address the barriers that have been discovered. As the goal-setting team discusses which barrier will be targeted, the student and teacher should discuss what is within the student that is contributing to the barrier. If the student is struggling with an intrapersonal issue, the teacher can choose from the activities and resources available in Chapter 5: Know

Thyself. If the student is struggling with an interpersonal skill, the teacher can choose from the activities and resources available in Chapter 6: Express Thyself. These interventions can be used in the mentoring time with gifted and high-potential students to help strengthen their weaknesses and give them ideas for tackling barriers. These interventions, however, are not the totality of the PEGS Model. These should be used as a supplement to the goal setting the student is regularly doing.

Perpetual PEGS Process

PEGS is an ongoing goal-setting process with reflection being a catalyst for the next goal. The Purposeful Empowerment in Goal Setting Workspace A and B (see Resources 8.2 and 8.3) is organized to follow the process of identifying strengths and areas for growth, identifying the barrier the student is struggling with, then analyzing through intrapersonal and interpersonal awareness, applying this to their learning, and reflecting on the outcome.

RESOURCE 8.2
Purposeful Empowerment in Goal Setting Workspace (A)

Name: _____

Areas of Strength: _____

Areas for Growth: _____

What's the Barrier?	Know Thyself Identify Strengths and Areas for Growth	Express Thyself Communicate, Problem-Solve, Advocate	Apply Thyself Desired Outcome
Let's reflect: Did you achieve the desired outcome? If not, what part of the process was the problem?			

155

RESOURCE 8.3

Purposeful Empowerment in Goal Setting Workspace (B)

Name: _____

Next area to target: _____

What's the Barrier?		**Know Thyself** Identify Strengths and Areas for Growth	**Express Thyself** Communicate, Problem-Solve, Advocate	**Apply Thyself** Desired Outcome
Let's reflect: Did you achieve the desired outcome? If not, what part of the process was the problem?				

Next area to target: _____

What's the Barrier?		**Know Thyself** Idertify Strengths & Areas for Growth	**Express Thyself** Communicate, Problem-Solve, Advocate	**Apply Thyself** Desired Outcome
Let's reflect: Did you achieve the desired outcome? If not, what part of the process was the problem?				

Purposeful Empowerment in Goal Setting Workspace

When beginning PEGS, the teacher should first provide students with the PEGS Workspace (A). The following sections outline the use of this resource.

1. With this resource, gifted and high-potential students begin by acknowledging their strengths. Having opportunities to be reminded of what they do well encourages students to want to grow in other areas. Students then reflect on things they may have difficulty with in the Areas for Growth section. Growth areas should align with what the student has logged as "barriers" on the Assessments Analysis. These areas do not need to be tackled all at once. Recording them in this section gives the student a choice as to what they would like to work on and set a goal toward.

2. In the middle section of the *Purposeful Empowerment in Goal Setting Workspace*, the student and teacher identify the barrier the student would like to focus on for that session. The teacher and student discuss what the student would like to see happen and record this in the Apply Thyself section. The Apply Thyself (i.e., desired outcome) section can also be completed as a final step in the process. However, discussing the desired outcome before problem-solving can be useful because the student knows exactly what they are working toward. This gives them the destination before they create the roadmap.

3. In the Know Thyself (i.e., intrapersonal) section, the student and teacher discuss what is within the student that is contributing to the barrier and what traits can help overcome the barrier.

4. In the Express Thyself (i.e., interpersonal) section, the teacher guides the student on how they might communicate, problem-solve, or advocate for themself to overcome the barrier. This is the student's action plan. When they leave the PEGS conference, the student will use what they have discussed and written in the Know Thyself and Express Thyself sections to develop the Apply Thyself desired outcome.

5. At the next conference, the student reflects on how the action plan played out. They discuss what went right, what did not go so well, and if the desired outcome was achieved. If the desired outcome was achieved, the teacher and student celebrate the progress the student has made. The small success of achieving this goal is a drop in the bucket of building resilience.

Resource 8.3

Purposeful Empowerment in Goal Setting Workspace (B)
Next area to target: ___Having a better understanding of Algebra II concepts___

What's the Barrier?	Know Thyself Identify Strengths and Areas for Growth	Express Thyself Communicate, Problem-Solve, Advocate	Apply Thyself Desired Outcome
Not fully understanding the concept which causes small mistakes on assignments and tests	I'm a quick-learner and motivated to do well in all classes; I don't pay attention to the small details	Review my notes before completing assignments; note small details of each algebraic equation	Having a full understanding of Algebra II in order to apply the knowledge to the ACT

Let's reflect: Did you achieve the desired outcome? If not, what part of the process was the problem?
I have been working toward this goal by reviewing my notes regularly. I have had some makeup work to do lately, but reviewing my notes is helping me complete the additional work.

Next area to target: ___Setting a routine for studying for the ACT___

Figure 8.1 Sample PEGS Workspace

6. If the goal was not achieved and the desired outcome not realized, the teacher and student discuss tweaks that should be made in order to achieve this goal.

7. PEGS Workspace (A) is used within the first few sessions, in order to build the habit of thinking about the student's strengths at the beginning of the goal-setting process. The teacher and student use PEGS Workspace (B) once the student is familiar with the process.

8. PEGS Workspace (B) is a pared-down version of the PEGS process. This resource is one that can be easily photocopied by the teacher and made ready for each conference session. Because the process is repeated in each session, it is more easily accessible in the shortened format. The student can also easily see the previous goal and reflection. The previous goal may drive the next goal, and past information can be beneficial in developing new plans of action. Students use the teacher's feedback and their own thoughts/feelings to set goals and create plans of action. Student agency is built as they take ownership of their actions and not merely let life happen to them. See Figure 8.1 for an example of the use of PEGS Workspace (B) with a student.

Reflection

Reflection is one of the key components of the PEGS Model. Without self-reflection, gifted and high-potential students' goals would be arbitrary and lack purpose. The student would only be filling in the sections of the graphic organizer just because a teacher told them to. Reflection is the piece of the puzzle that makes Purposeful Empowerment in Goal Setting *purposeful*. Just like seeing their reflection in a mirror, the student will use the ongoing reflection opportunities to examine their true self.

Many gifted and high-potential students do not think about who they are and why they take the actions they do. There is no real purpose to their young lives, as they are following the plan that society has set for them. When a student is reflective on their own, they usually only look at their performance in a sport or on an exam. But scoring a goal in soccer or an 87% on an exam does not give the student the information they need to recognize their strengths and improve their performance. Gifted and high-potential students must learn to reflect on the entire process and use that data to formulate new goals.

Reflecting On Who They Are

Reflection is found in several sections of the PEGS Model. Gifted and high-potential students will begin reflecting as they respond to the prompts in the intrapersonal and interpersonal assessments. These insights into themselves allow students to take a look at their performance and behaviors and explore the motivations and attitudes behind them. To extend this look in the mirror further, students will reflect on the assessments as a whole with the reflection questions after each assessment. It is recommended that the student discuss these questions with their teacher. The teacher can offer insight within the student reflection or help the student to make connections to what is happening. These reflective times will inform the student's Assessments Analysis (see Resource 5.1) and drive their goals.

Reflecting on Their Skills

Gifted and high-potential students are also prompted to reflect within the intrapersonal and interpersonal interventions offered in Chapters 5 and 6. As they explore and improve in these areas, it is important for them to note where they are in the process of learning and celebrate the progress they have made. Reflection makes the celebration and understanding possible. The teacher should offer the reflection questions when the intervention is complete and make a point to discuss the questions with the student. If these interventions are done in a whole group setting, the teacher should have the students respond in writing and then conference with them one-on-one at a different time. Discussion with a mentor sheds light on things the student may not have realized. Moments of realization through reflection will drive the student's goals and their ability to solve problems to overcome their barriers.

Reflecting on Their Progress

Finally, gifted and high-potential students are prompted at the beginning of each PEGS session to reflect on the outcome of the short-term goal they set previously. Reflection at the beginning of the conference reminds students of the goal they have set, gives them opportunities to trouble-shoot with the teacher if they have difficulties, and holds them accountable. Students receive feedback and insight from the teacher when they are honest about their anxiety, procrastination, or not knowing where to start. The best part of reflection in each goal, though, is that many times it starts the session off with celebration. It is very exciting for students to share their small wins with their teacher.

Reflection in the goal-setting process also serves as the catalyst for the next goal. If the student sets a goal and then forgets about it, the student can reflect on why they forgot to carry out the tasks. The teacher and student can problem-solve through this and set a new goal to by-pass this barrier. If the student sets a goal and has trouble completing it because they were nervous or anxious, the teacher and student can refer back to the student's intrapersonal strengths and build the goal based on what the student feels comfortable doing. If the student sets a goal and then has trouble in an area of communication, the teacher and student can refer back to the student's interpersonal skills, review their strengths, and add in interventions to overcome the communication barrier. As gifted and high-potential students reflect on the goal, the information gleaned will drive them to hone in on what needs to happen or move on to the next goal. Self-reflection makes this goal-setting process purposeful and empowering to students.

Tips for Implementing PEGS

During the PEGS sessions, there may be things that come up that could be frustrating for the teacher or students. There may also be times when the teacher can draw from their own experiences to guide them on what they should do. It is important, though, for the teacher to teach through stories or suggestions and not tell the students exactly what to do. The teacher is mentoring students in this process. The teacher can lead gifted and high-potential students to a solution and build the capacity within them to solve future problems on their own. Table 8.3 provides a few tips for implementing PEGS with gifted and high-potential students.

Success with PEGS

The PEGS Model was developed for use with students in a personalized setting, as there was nothing like it available. Below are a few snippets of successes that have been seen from students, ranging in age from 5th to 12th grade. The PEGS Model is versatile in its use because it meets each student where they are.

TABLE 8.3
Tips for Implementing PEGS

Tips for Implementing PEGS
• Encourage students to stick with goals that are useful to their education and social relationships. While it is admirable to set goals for extracurriculars and hobbies, the PEGS time should be set aside for empowering the student in their education.
• Students tend to perseverate on all-or-nothing thinking. Guide the student to understand that a little progress toward the goal is better than not trying at all. Have the student strive to get 1% better each day.
• Students can become overwhelmed by large goals (e.g., research projects, applications). The teacher should model how to break large goals down into smaller, attainable tasks. The use of a to-do list or calendar can be helpful in showing examples of this.
• Students can get wrapped up in logistics and terminology which can sometimes stifle productivity. They might not complete the goal if they can't do it exactly as written. The teacher should model flexibility and the use of more general terms. For example: "I will complete my homework when I get home from school" instead of "I will complete my homework from 4:30–6:00 pm."
• Take time to draw from your own experiences to guide the student. Giving the students real-life scenarios the teacher has encountered shows them they are not alone in this situation. When the teacher shares part of their life, they will also foster a trusting relationship with the student.

Understanding of Why

A student who is profoundly gifted and extremely talented in the area of mathematics was struggling in his math class. During his PEGS session, he would regularly bring up the difficulties he was having in his class, stating that he already knew the material and found he was quite uninterested in wasting his time reviewing it. He had been given the recommendation of finding a way to tell the teacher he already knew the material several times. The student never seemed to be able to communicate with her about receiving more challenging work. As he worked through PEGS with his gifted education teacher, he came to the realization that he was not advocating for himself due to the fact he was not turning in the work the teacher assigned. He revealed that he was ashamed and embarrassed for getting poor grades due to not handing in assignments and felt that the teacher would not give him more challenging work because of this. The student used this new knowledge of himself gleaned through the PEGS process to convey the feelings he was having and worked with his teacher to find a way to advocate for more challenging instruction.

Quashing Anxiety

During a PEGS session, another student voiced high anxiety in performing in front of others. She experienced this inner turmoil in class when the teacher called on her, and she never volunteered to answer aloud despite having the highest grade in the class. She also refused to be the leader in group work, step out for any activity that would put her in the spotlight, or work on skills in front of her peers. During the abilities assessments, this student found that she places high value on success and friendship. Because of these values, she never wants her friends to see her not be successful. As she talked through this with her gifted education teacher, the teacher posed the question, "Do your friends really care if you make a mistake in math?" The student talked through a scenario where she might get the answer wrong and what would happen if she did. She had never thought through this to the end to see that mistakes do not matter to her friends. They like her because of who she is. She also realized that making a mistake could help her improve in math, a subject she values a lot. She eventually set goals using the PEGS process that would highlight situations where she would need to perform in front of others and employed the "Who cares if I mess up?" mentality. In her reflections, she celebrated each time she overcame a social anxiety barrier and took a small risk to get better at something.

Finding Voice

Another student used PEGS to confront the issue of not getting his homework completed and turned in. This was negatively affecting his grades. During discussion with his gifted education teacher, he stated that his mother would make him do his homework immediately after coming home from school. While sequestered in his room, he might work a little, but then get distracted by his phone or computer. When it was time for dinner, he would be set free and spend the rest of his night playing video games. Essentially, he would get nothing done. He realized that he has difficulty concentrating for long periods of time and really needed a break to decompress after school. He did not think that his mother's homework rule would change, so he never thought to talk about it. After some discussion on what to say, he used the perpetual PEGS Model to set a goal. He planned to talk to his mom about changing her homework policy to allow him some time to relax before getting started on homework. In reflection, the student found that talking to his mother about this one issue opened the door for him to advocate more for himself in the future.

Promoting Success with PEGS

Use of the PEGS Model with gifted and high-potential students continues to show great success. These successes come in many areas of the students' lives. The students are learning about who they are and how their actions affect their futures, whether it's tomorrow or years down the line. Students are seeing that their choices are a vote for who they want to be and what they want to do in this world. It is helping them to see that they are the main character in the story they are writing for themselves. Success has also come in the lives of the teachers who implement PEGS. In reflection with students, teachers consequently reflect on their own behaviors and are inspired toward change, inside and outside of the classroom. The main success of PEGS implementation is the relationships that are formed between teacher and student. The lives of both are impacted and made better by the honesty and respect that is maintained. The student is seen as a valuable contributor to society by the teacher. The teacher is seen as a valuable mentor to the student. Overall, Purposeful Empowerment in Goal Setting can be the catalyst for improvement in many areas of the lives of students, giving them the tools they need to succeed in our global world.

References

Cavilla, D. (2019). Maximizing the potential of gifted learners through a development framework of affective curriculum. *Gifted Education International, 35*(2), 136–151. http://dx.doi.org/10.1177/026142941 8821875

Rakow, S. (2020). *Educating gifted students in middle school.* Routledge.

Siegel, D. J., & Payne Bryson, T. (2012). *The whole-brain child: 12 revolutionary strategies to nurture your child's developing mind.* Robinson.

Sousa, D. A. (2009). *How the gifted brain learns.* Corwin.

Wehmeyer, M. (2002, September). *Self-determination and the education of students with disabilities.* Hoagies' Gifted Education. www.hoagiesgifted.org/eric/e632.html

CHAPTER 9

Goal Setting in High School and Beyond

It is no secret that the high school experience is a challenging one. Students encounter many changes and challenges throughout their time in high school, all while also navigating changing bodies and minds. Gifted and high-potential students are not immune to these challenges. It could be said that because of their sensitivity to their environment and intensity of feelings, a gifted or high-potential student may be more susceptible to issues in a high school environment. The goal of this chapter is to explore some potential barriers gifted and high-potential learners may encounter in the high school setting and how Purposeful Empowerment in Goal Setting (PEGS) can address these areas.

Social-Emotional Characteristics

Gifted and high-potential students in the high school setting continue to have the propensity to be creative and critical thinkers, enjoy abstract challenges, and pursue their interests. However, in high school, they can finally see the finish line of their K-12 experience. The pressure of completing the high school coursework, along with all the other demands of a high school student, can be overwhelming. Gifted and high-potential students come into high school with a heightened awareness of the

DOI: 10.4324/9781003331049-10

expectations others have for them and increased ability to criticize their own performance (Alodat et al., 2020; Cross, 1997). They can begin doubting themselves and feel inadequate in their pursuits (Piechowski, 1997). While many gifted and high-potential students have the self-regulation skills and resiliency needed to move past these feelings and continue to achieve, some students may experience low motivation, feel isolated from their peers, and encounter mental health issues. It is important for students to develop the skills necessary to overcome these challenges as they progress to the next stages of life.

Academic Expectations

Rigorous academic expectations from themselves, peers, teachers, and parents can cause gifted and high-potential learners undue stress. As students enter into high school, and even when they are registering for freshman classes while still in eighth grade, they are asked to choose the path they would like to take. More than ever, students are being offered and actively seeking accelerated courses that either offer college credit or prepare them for college classes (Suldo et al., 2018). Making the choices about which courses to take and how rigorous they should be can be a stressor in itself. When the students are in these courses, the expectations to achieve in grades and on exams press on them further. Students in accelerated curricula experience a much higher level of stress than students in standard courses (Suldo, et al., 2018). Gifted and high-potential learners should be given opportunities to explore the goals they have for their education and strategies for coping with the stress that comes with high achievement.

Healthy and Unhealthy Perfectionism

Gifted and high-potential students hold themselves to a standard above the norm. They generally enjoy achieving and striving toward their idea of perfection. This can be considered healthy and adaptive perfectionism. If a student shows signs of healthy perfectionism, it is important for them to learn how to continue to channel this to be successful. However, if a student experiences unhealthy perfectionism, they could begin to exhibit maladaptive behaviors such as anxiety, difficulty with peers and in social situations, and other mental health issues (Mofield & Parker Peters, 2018). Perfectionism, whether viewed by practitioners as positive or negative, is a trait that should be addressed with gifted and high-potential students as they are managing their high school careers. If not addressed, issues may arise with the student that could be detrimental to their academic pursuits and within their lives.

Fixed and Growth Mindset

Gifted and high-potential learners who are entering high school have no doubt been told they are smart many times in their lives. Throughout their school careers, students have cultivated a mindset that holds their beliefs about how and if they can reach their potential (Esparza et al., 2014). When a student believes that their intelligence can change and grow, they are considered to have a growth mindset (Dweck, 2012). Students with a growth mindset can use feedback, increase their effort, and improve their performance. A growth mindset also allows a student to understand that they do not know everything and each opportunity presents new information. However, a student with a fixed mindset believes that their intelligence cannot change (Dweck, 2012).

Gifted and high-potential students with a fixed mindset may only attempt challenges that look easy or good in the eyes of their peers. They may have little resilience in the face of setbacks and quit the task altogether. Students with a fixed mindset may not understand that their only motivation comes from the perception others have of them. A fixed mindset can put up several barriers for a high school gifted or high-potential learner. They may find that when the classes get harder, they have less motivation to pursue the challenges. They may also find that they are only pursuing the goals that others have set for them, and they no longer have interest in pursuing these. It is key for gifted and high-potential students to recognize what type of mindset they hold about their potential and make the necessary changes in order for them to succeed.

Uncertainty and Future Goals

To a high school student, the future may be this broad and vast concept that they are striving toward. They may have no real direction or plan for the future. Many times, high school students only see the finish line of graduation and do not consider what lies beyond. While some gifted and high-potential students do fall into this category, others may have their futures planned out in heavy detail. They may know exactly what colleges they will apply to, when they plan to apply, what majors they will pursue, and the career path they will follow. High school graduation day for these students is merely the beginning. In either case, students should have some assistance in setting, planning, and implementing the steps toward their future goals. Both types of students and all who fall in between will experience some anxiety and uncertainty as they embark on their journey. It is important for these students to have supports in place to guide them through the steps.

Impact of PEGS in High School

Purposeful Empowerment in Goal Setting can have a great impact on the lives of gifted and high-potential high school students. This goal-setting process can be implemented during consultation, counseling services, or other times in the student's school day. The PEGS process requires the teacher to develop a respectful relationship with the student and become the student's coach in goal setting. The teacher and student should first work through the abilities assessments provided in Chapter 4 to help the student realize their traits, values, and motivations, and gain awareness of their strengths and weaknesses. The teacher and student then identify the needs of the student and set short-term goals to make a positive impact in the areas identified. The result increases the student's intrapersonal awareness, interpersonal skills, and their ability to apply these to their learning. Below are some examples of where the PEGS process can achieve positive outcomes with gifted and high-potential students in the high school setting.

❏ Increased student self-awareness
❏ Development of self-regulation skills
❏ Adoption of a growth mindset
❏ Identifying stakeholders and advocating for themselves

Student Self-Awareness

A car fresh off the showroom floor will be expected to run in tip-top shape for quite a while. Brand new cars should accelerate easily, brake well, and be responsive to the driver. However, if something were to stop working correctly, the car's indicator lights would turn on, making the driver aware of the issue. If there were no indicator lights to let the driver know of the problem, the car's issues could possibly render it unable to perform. Gifted and high-potential students tend to be perceived as high-performing vehicles without any need for maintenance. They are expected to achieve at high levels in rigorous classes and to know exactly how to manage all that goes with them. When something is not exactly right within these students though, there is no indicator light to make them aware of the potential problem. Students can possibly develop unhealthy coping mechanisms, procrastination, and/or underachievement if the expectations are becoming too much. They may not even realize that these things are happening within themselves.

In order for a gifted student to understand what is happening within themself, they must develop self-awareness. The intrapersonal and interpersonal assessments in Chapter 4 can act as the indicator light for the student to recognize their performance status. They may realize that all systems are working well and recognize what they are doing in order to achieve at a high level. They may also realize through these assessments that some components are not functioning correctly. It is possible that a student's values are out of alignment with their goals. The student may be lacking in motivation or fail to see the value in the tasks they are required to complete. Students may realize they are not resilient when faced with challenges or have difficulty managing their time and materials. Developing this self-awareness is the first step in the student setting purposeful goals. With the assessments as indicator lights for students, they can then develop a plan for maintenance in that area and apply the new skills to their performance.

Developing Self-Regulation

As referenced in Chapter 2, a self-regulated learner is one who recognizes their needs and distractions from their goals, uses appropriate coping strategies, and is aware of what they need to be successful (Cash, 2016). High school is a time in a student's life when these skills are necessary. The increase in rigor of concepts, large amounts of homework, and navigating a more autonomous environment can increase the anxiety of gifted and high-potential students. The increased anxiety can cause feelings in each situation to bubble up and may initiate an unintended reaction from the student. The student must learn to recognize their feelings, understand what behavior is stemming from their emotions, and use this understanding to analyze their thoughts on the situation (Cash, 2016). This procedure is instrumental in helping the student change the story they are telling themself and find a way to overcome the barrier. The PEGS Model is designed to give the gifted and high-potential student opportunities to explore how they are feeling, what is internally and externally causing these feelings, and to devise a plan to work through this. A learner with self-regulation strategies in their toolbelt can easily locate and repair the issue. Increased motivation and effort may even follow if the student is able to regulate their emotions within a challenge and persist in seeing it through.

Adopting a Growth Mindset

The mind is a powerful tool. It can make or break someone. It can easily defeat a person or be stronger than any physical muscle. Realizing the power of their mind is an important part of a student setting goals and following through with them. The story students tell themselves is what drives their mindset. If students are telling themselves that they are smart only when the task is easy, they will only try tasks they cannot fail in. If they regularly tell themselves that their ideas or opinions are not as good as someone else's, they will never step out and show what they are capable of. If students tell themselves that they must perfectly follow the plan others have set for them, their idea of who they really are will diminish. The PEGS process can help to break the cycle of the gifted student continuously telling themself that a skewed story is true. In using the PEGS process, the student is faced with their real and true story. They are given the opportunity to discover why they are telling themself something different than the truth. They will be given a chance to put systems in place to overcome the false story and live as their authentic self.

Achieving a growth mindset may be a difficult task for high school students since they have potentially gone through so many years of school with the same thought processes. It is not easy to break the habit. In order to break the cycle of using a fixed mindset, the student has to first take action. The student must get to know themself and then set easily attainable goals. The action they take toward that goal will cause more action. The student should intentionally reflect on their progress and make the connection to how the progress is impacting the story they would like to tell about themself.

As they regularly set achievable goals and follow through with them, they are beginning to adopt more of a growth mindset. They begin to see that they can learn new things and that it is ok if they do not have all the answers. They can see progress toward something they do not have yet but will eventually get. They will begin to see that how others perceive them does not matter as long as they are taking the next right step. PEGS is an amazing pathway to lead students to a growth mindset and becoming lifelong improvers.

Identifying Stakeholders in High School

As students enter into the high school setting, many are unsure of who they can trust and who is there to support them. Gifted and high-potential students are often unprepared for the amount of autonomy needed in this setting. If they are directed and supported in identifying who has a stake in their education and therefore wants to help them succeed, they can quickly learn how and when to advocate for themselves in a positive way. By definition, a stakeholder is any person in an organization who can have an effect on achievement (Freeman, 2004). Gifted and high-potential students should have opportunities to explore the people involved in their lives and education and how those stakeholders can support them. In the following section, an overview of stakeholders within the high school setting will be reviewed as they pertain to the time period the student needs them. The PEGS Model is a channel for guiding the student to advocate for themself and identifying and understanding who is in their corner is a significant component to that process.

Transitioning to High School (End of 8th Grade/ 9th Grade)

The task of registering for high school can be extremely daunting and anxiety producing for gifted and high-potential students. There is much uncertainty in what their future holds. Using the PEGS process, students voice these concerns with their trusted teacher and work through a plan of action. In this process, the teacher offers a list of stakeholders students can contact or receive guidance from in order to alleviate some of the stress and anxiety in this situation. Beginning with the teacher students are already working with, a list of these stakeholders may include the student's parents, the middle school guidance counselor, a trusted general education teacher with knowledge of the high school curriculum, the district's gifted specialist, and the high school guidance counselor. Each of these stakeholders can listen to student questions or concerns and offer advice in their area of expertise. It is important to note that students may feel uneasy talking to these people or may have difficulty knowing what to say. The use of the PEGS process is a great way to coach these skills. The student can set the small goal of meeting with the stakeholder and

TABLE 9.1

Stakeholders in the High School Setting

Building-Level Stakeholders	Classroom-Level Stakeholders	Community-Level Stakeholders
• School Attendance Clerk • School Secretary • Librarian/LRC Director • Guidance Counselors • Social Workers • Assistant Principal • School Principal • School Resource Officer	• Current Teachers • Former Teachers • Gifted Specialists • Student Leaders • Club/Sports Sponsors	• Sports Coaches • Extracurricular Instructors • School Board Members • Family • Community Business Owners • Spiritual Leaders

problem-solve through the scenario with the teacher before the scheduled encounter.

Once the students have entered into freshman year, the teacher should also provide a list of stakeholders in this new setting. Freshman year of high school is full of new experiences and new faces. Students may be in a new building with a schedule to navigate. They may not know anyone in their classes. It will be of great benefit for the student if they know a few adults in the building they can go to if needed. Having a list of teachers, support staff, administrators, and guidance counselors ready will give comfort to the anxious student and create more confidence in their ability to succeed in those first weeks. This list will also come in handy as students encounter scenarios where they must advocate for themselves. Table 9.1 provides examples of stakeholders who may be important for students to know.

Self-Advocacy Throughout High School

Self-advocacy can be thought of as the student taking ownership of their education by recognizing their needs and communicating these needs to specific stakeholders. Self-advocacy also continues to be a contributing factor in growing student agency. The PEGS process can be an ideal tool for encouraging high school students toward advocating for themselves. Gifted and high-potential students can be timid when asking questions or seeking guidance, as they do not want to be perceived as not being smart. They can be hesitant to talk with a teacher about more challenging material when they are not performing at their best in the class. They may also lack the communication skills necessary to tactfully or fully communicate with an adult.

As the teacher and student use the PEGS Model to develop goals in these areas, the teacher should talk through scenarios for identifying the needs of the student and ways to communicate these needs to stakeholders who can help. There are four essential steps for gifted and high-potential learners to take to be successful in advocating for themselves: understanding their own rights and responsibilities, understanding their own personal attributes, finding the options that match what is meaningful for them, and making connections with stakeholders who can help with their plan (Douglas, 2018). This process can easily follow the Purposeful Empowerment in Goal Setting Model, as the student is working through their intrapersonal awareness, interpersonal skills, and applying this knowledge to their learning and environment.

As the student begins to advocate for themself, it is important to address their responsibilities in the classroom. If a student feels that they are not being challenged in the classroom because they already know the material, they must be able to find a way to communicate this to their teacher. However, many students become bored or uninterested when they are not given challenging material (Hoekman et al., 2005). This can cause complacency and a lack of motivation to complete assigned work. While the teacher should differentiate instruction, it is the student's responsibility to *first* show what they know by completing assigned work and *then* to ask for challenges. Other responsibilities a student has in the classroom include being on time for class, showing respect for both teacher and peers, and having necessary materials. If gifted and high-potential students can understand and perform their responsibilities, their teachers will be more likely to listen when they self-advocate.

Gifted and high-potential students must also learn what their rights are in the school setting. Students have the right to make choices for themselves when it comes to coursework and academic paths. Many students believe they must take only the classes that are on a specific path or have been chosen by their parents or guidance counselor. Students should be encouraged to read the school handbook and understand what courses are actually offered and in what order they may be taken. Students who use the PEGS process will also be able to hone in on which courses excite them and which courses would best fit into their long-term goals. This is also a way for them to find what works best for them and create a plan to achieve it.

In order to fully carry out self-advocacy, the student must connect with the stakeholders who can impact their achievement. The PEGS

Model gives the student the tools needed to be successful in communication. With coaching from their trusted teacher, gifted and high-potential students work through scenarios, role play conversations, and make detailed plans for discussing their needs with these stakeholders. In the case of planning classes for the following year, the student works with the teacher to identify what is most important to them and what they value most for the upcoming semester, analyze what classes fit best with these, and make a plan for setting the schedule. The student can then also have discussions with their parents and other trusted teachers and finally discuss the courses with their guidance counselor. The student will have worked through the situation prior to speaking with the stakeholders. This forethought and planning will give the student confidence to convey their needs and propose a plan that works for them. Having the skill of self-advocacy will empower the student to take ownership of their future.

Transitioning Out of High School

The transition out of high school is an exciting occasion that can also be terrifying to a student. There are hundreds of tasks to be completed, decisions to make, essays to write, applications to complete, and opportunities to seek. While it may be the job of the student to continue to drive this train, they will need some help along the way. The last year of high school is a crucial time for gifted and high-potential students to advocate for themselves. The trusted teacher should be the student's guide through this process. Reminding the student of stakeholders who can impact and influence decisions should be a top priority for the teacher. At this point in their high school career, the student should have made some excellent teacher contacts within the school. These teachers will have knowledge of the student and can provide information about specific programs and scholarships. They can also be asked to write recommendation letters for the student. The student's guidance counselor will be an integral part of the student's college application process, as well as learning about scholarships, important exams, and upcoming deadlines. The teacher can also remind the student to seek stakeholders outside of their school building. The student may find jobs or internships within the community, and the contacts made there can lead to other opportunities. The student's parents and family are also stakeholders who can be of benefit and support in this time of transition. The teacher and student will be able work through scenarios using the PEGS Model while they set goals for the end of their high school career.

Areas of Focus in High School Using PEGS

When implementing the Purposeful Empowerment in Goal Setting Model with students in high school, there are a few areas of focus that may be specific to each grade level. Table 9.2 provides examples of these areas by grade level. It is important for gifted and high-potential students entering high school and completing freshman year to first have a good understanding of themselves. They must have the self-awareness to understand their strengths and weaknesses in the classroom, in relationships, and within themselves. They must also be able to navigate the school building, course progressions, and the stakeholders involved. Students in their sophomore year of high school are more settled in the school building and are navigating harder coursework. They must build good habits in time management and study skills in order to boost their achievement. They may also need support in locating leadership opportunities and continuing to study for important

TABLE 9.2
Using PEGS Throughout High School

High School Grade Level	Skills and Areas to Address with PEGS
Freshman Year/9th Grade	Work through the PEGS Model beginning with intrapersonal awareness; school building resources; course progressions; stakeholders
Sophomore Year/10th Grade	Continuing PEGS Model, focusing on time management and study skills; leadership and/or community involvement; prepping for and/or taking AP exams, the ACT/SAT
Junior Year/11th Grade	Applying PEGS to personal goals or after high school goals; motivations and goals that influence college and career choices; community involvement (e.g., part-time jobs, volunteer work, driver's license exam)
Senior Year/12th Grade	Use PEGS to guide planning the college application process, college/scholarship essays, completing college applications, and preparing for interviews

exams such as AP (Advanced Placement) or IB (International Baccalaureate) exams and the ACT/SAT. Junior-year students are beginning to realize that the end of their high school career is near. These students will need support in applying the PEGS Model toward their high school goals, which may include a certain GPA or specific amount of accelerated courses. This may be a time for the student to use their knowledge of their own skills and motivations to prompt exploration of colleges and career paths. Students may also need support in getting a part-time job and preparing for their driver's license. Finally, senior year presents the opportunity for support in choosing colleges to apply to, planning the college application process, setting goals for essays and deadlines, and preparing for college interviews. Table 9.2 gives an outline of each grade level and possible skills to address in the PEGS process. The teacher and student should set short-term, easily attainable goals that empower the student to follow through to their dreams.

PEGS Through High School and Beyond

It is the specific goal of the PEGS Model to empower students to understand and reflect on who they are, how they interact with the world, how these apply to their achievement, and to set purposeful goals that fall in line with these. As gifted and high-potential students are empowered in goal setting through this model, they begin to develop self-awareness, which increases their confidence and motivation. They are able to self-regulate in all situations and effectively communicate with the people around them. They begin to understand that they are in control of their lives and their choices make things happen. Goal setting with the PEGS Model can become a habit and then become internalized with continuous use. When the learner has internalized this process and taken ownership of their life, they will be able to set goals, make decisions for themself, and confidently take on adulthood. It is the hope of all teachers working with gifted and high-potential students that they will become productive citizens of the world and fully reach their potential. Purposeful Empowerment in Goal Setting can be the precise tool needed to see this hope through.

References

Alodat, A., Abu, G., Moawyah, M., & Al-Hamouri, F.A. (2020). Perfectionism and academic self-handicapped among gifted students: An explanatory mode. *International Journal of Educational Psychology, 9*(2), 195–222. https://doi.org/10.17583/ijep.2020.4426

Cash, R. M. (2016). *Self-regulation in the classroom: Helping students learn how to learn.* Free Spirit Press.

Cross, T. L. (1997). Psychological and social aspects of educating gifted students. *Peabody Journal of Education, 72*(3), 180–200. https://doi.org/10.1207/s15327930pje7203&4_11

Douglas, D. (2018). *Self-advocacy tip sheet.* National Association for Gifted Children. www.nagc.org/sites/default/files/Publication%20PHP/NAGC-TIP%20SHEET-Self%20Advocacy.pdf

Dweck, C. S. (2012). Mindsets and human nature: Promoting change in the Middle East, the schoolyard, the racial divide, and willpower. *American Psychologist, 67*(8), 614–622. https://doi.org/10.1037/a0029783

Esparza, J., Shumow, L., & Schmidt, J. A. (2014). Growth mindset of gifted seventh grade students in science. *National Consortium of Secondary STEM Schools Journal, 19*(1), 6–13.

Freeman, R. E. (2004). The stakeholder approach revisited. *Zeitschrift Für Wirtschafts- Und Unternehmensethik, 5*(3), 228–254. https://doi.org/10.5771/1439-880x-2004-3-228

Hoekman, K., McCormick, J., & Barnett, K. (2005). The important role of optimism in a motivational investigation of the education of gifted adolescents. *Gifted Child Quarterly, 49*(2), 99–110.

Mofield, E. L., & Parker Peters, M. (2018). Shifting the perfectionistic mindset: Moving to mindful excellence. *Gifted Child Today, 41*(4), 177–185.

Piechowski, M. M. (1997). Emotional giftedness: The measure of intrapersonal intelligence. In N. Colangelo & G. A. Davis (Eds.), *Handbook of gifted education* (2nd ed., pp. 366–381). Allyn & Bacon.

Suldo, S. M., O'Brennan, L., Storey, E. D., & Shaunessy-Dedrick, E. (2018). Supporting high school students in accelerated courses. *Communique, 46*(6), 18–21.

Conclusion and Final Thoughts

After years of teaching gifted and high-potential students, we knew it was becoming more and more important to turn the focus toward our students instead of toward instruction. Our students were needing support in understanding themselves and the world around them. They were being blamed for not already knowing how to handle their emotions, tasks, and needs. Their ways of thinking were often getting in the way of their learning. Tich Nhat Hanh (2016), a Zen Buddhist monk, teacher, and peace activist said, "When you plant lettuce, if it does not grow well, you don't blame the lettuce. You look into the reasons it is not doing well." We knew we needed to get to the root of what was happening within our students so they could grow, thrive, and flourish.

Nhất Hanh goes on to say, "No blame, no reasoning, no argument, just understanding. If you understand, and you show that you understand, you can love, and the situation will change." Purposeful Empowerment in Goal Setting (PEGS) has led to the understanding our students need and deserve. Our students now understand themselves more fully through their development in intrapersonal awareness. They are able to help the people around them better understand who they are through their communication and self-advocacy skills. They better understand their needs in the classroom and in life and then problem-solve through these needs. Our students have begun to bloom. It is our hope that PEGS can be used

DOI: 10.4324/9781003331049-11

with gifted and high-potential students around the world in order for them to be able to develop the self-awareness and student agency necessary to achieve their goals. We would like every student's potential to be recognized and brought to fruition from this process. It is our hope that through the use of the PEGS Model, gifted and high-potential students will no longer be the square peg in the round hole, but climb the ladder of success and have a positive influence in our global world.

Reference

Nhất Hạnh, T. (2016). *At home in the world: Stories and essential teachings from a monk's life*. Parallax Press.

About the Authors

Vicki Phelps is an Assistant Professor of Education at Milligan University. She has been involved in gifted education for 25 years and enjoys providing professional learning and consultation services to districts seeking to improve gifted practice. Dr. Phelps is the recipient of the 2021 NAGC Book of the Year Award (with Emily Mofield) for *Collaboration, Coteaching, and Coaching in Gifted Education*. In addition to her published research on gifted motivation, her work is also included in *The New Teacher's Guide to Overcoming Common Challenges*. She is the author of *Successful Online Learning with Gifted Students* and looks forward to her upcoming new release, *Coaching in Gifted Education* (with Emily Mofield).

Karah Lewis is the Lead Consulting Teacher for Gifted Education and the county-wide Gifted Consultant for high school students in Sumner County, Tennessee. She has a Bachelor's degree in Elementary Education (K-8) and a Master of Arts in Special Education (K-12). Karah has over 15 years of experience in the classroom, working with general education, special education, and gifted education. She enjoys developing curriculum and strategies to support gifted students and providing professional learning opportunities for teachers.